$\mathcal{U}$sing Art to Create Art

Creative Activities Using Masterpieces

Using Art to Create Art

Creative Activities Using Masterpieces

Wendy M. L. Libby

Delmar Staff:
Business Unit Director: Susan L. Simpfenderfer
Executive Editor: Marlene McHugh Pratt
Acquisitions Editor: Erin O'Connor Traylor
Developmental Editor: Melissa Riveglia
Editorial Assistant: Alexis Ferraro
Executive Production Manager: Wendy A. Troeger
Production Editor: Elaine Scull
Executive Marketing Manager: Donna Lewis
Channel Manager: Eleanor J. Murray
Cover Design: Joseph Villanova

COPYRIGHT © 2000
Delmar is a division of Thomson Learning. The Thomson Learning logo is a registered trademark used herein under license.

Printed in the United States of America
3 4 5 7 9 10 XXX 05

For more information, contact Delmar Learning, 5 Maxwell Drive, PO Box 8007, Clifton Park, NY 12065-2919;
or find us on the World Wide Web at http://www.delmarlearning.com or http://www.EarlyChildEd.delmar.com

Library of Congress Cataloging-in-Publication Data
Libby, Wendy M. L.
  Using art to make art: creative activities using masterpieces / Wendy M. L. Libby.
    p. cm.
  Includes bibliographical references and index.
  ISBN 0-7668-1505-6
  1. Art—Study and teaching (Elementary)—United States. I. Title

N362.L49 2000
372.5'044—dc21   99-054016
                                                   CIP

Dedication

To my husband, Bob, who is my strength; to my two sons, Brandon and Bradley, who are my inspiration; and to my parents, Arnold and Janice Leavitt, who taught me to believe in myself and follow my dreams.

Contents

Preface

This year marks the twenty-first year I have been teaching elementary art in the Bangor School Department in the state of Maine. During this time, I have taken part in the growth of the arts in our schools. When I began teaching I struggled with school budgets and the public's misconception that the arts were an area that could be cut. I am proud to say that this view has changed. Art is an integral part of my school system's curriculum. The strength of the visual has become valued across the curriculum. The study of art exposes children to particular methods of expression and inquiry and develops the verbal, perceptual, and imaginative skills needed to understand experiences.

An art experience should combine careful planning, spontaneous action, thinking, and feeling. Properly implemented, these elements can promote physical, mental, and aesthetic growth. Students should be encouraged to explore, experiment, and invent, in order to develop their creative imagination and thus contribute to their self-realization. Art allows children to visualize their experiences through imagination and feeling. They can use their art experiences as a means of measuring and understanding the quality of all experiences. Encouraging children to discover and appreciate what is in front of them will deepen their understanding of themselves, both as individuals and as members of society. Art experiences give children the opportunity to explore and experience the world in which they live, and guide them to respect and respond to it with originality and individuality. By practicing original thinking, doing, and evaluating, abstract ideas become easier for the students to visualize; this makes a vital contribution to their intellectual development. As they create their own responses to the world, students benefit from exposure to what artists have already created throughout history. The study of the master artists and their work assists in understanding the world as it was, is, and might be.

The lessons included in this book use the typical objectives of an elementary art curriculum and are based on the styles and techniques of master artists. Although one class may work on the same lesson activity, each student will add his or her own personal feelings and views to each of the lessons. The ideas for these lessons originated from studying the artists' work, from art books and art magazines, and from a very important teacher tool: other teachers. An artist's eyes are always observing, just as a teacher is always searching for ways to strengthen students' skills, knowledge, and creativity. All present and future teachers must realize the important impression they have on a child and continue to develop and share projects and lessons that are successful. This has been the basis for my conceptual approach to the development of the text. As a teacher I have successfully used these lessons in classrooms and with small groups, however, they are equally suited for parents and children at home. Lessons begin with discussions and demonstrations of the techniques to be used, then the children are allowed to complete the activity in their own individual way. An overview of the content of this book and its organization is explained in detail in the following section, About This Book.

The concept of utilizing the works of the masters to aquaint students with not only the wonders of art, but the practicality of it, is not totally original with this author. The individual lesson plans contained in this book provide a practical methodology to bring the study of art to every student, and should be valuable to all teachers who wish to include art content within their programs. This student-friendly approach to learning about art history and the styles and techniques of master artists has generated great enthusiasm for learning and sharing among the students. These methods have earned enthusiasm from parents as well. At student art shows, many parents have approached me with favorable comments regarding the introduction of their children to master artists and their varied styles of work. Feeling that the children are able to grasp the significance of the different art periods and appreciate what makes a style important and worthy of emulation is very gratifying and worthy of encouragement. Thus the endeavor of putting this book together.

After presenting a few lessons based on master artists and seeing the eagerness of the children to imitate the styles and techniques connected with these artists, I realized the excitement to review my own art history experiences was overwhelming. The feeling of being artists themselves was contagious and students began discussing the artists and their work with whatever information they were privy to. Impressed parents began commenting on how their children would notice reproductions hanging on walls in buildings, in books, on cards, or on stationery, and art discussions started taking place at home. I began to use more lessons on various artists as the students thirsted for more information. When I began gathering ideas for this book, I wanted to develop my curriculum to include the master artists and their work. This led to the creation of various lessons that were integrated with other areas of study, as other classroom teachers became excitedly involved. My first intent was to write down the lessons for other teachers to incorporate into their programs. Having supervised many student teachers from a nearby college, I realized the usefulness of a book of this type for anyone involved with teaching young children.

Acknowledgements

At this time, I want to thank all the educators who have strengthened my program, all the parents who have allowed me to teach and learn from their children, and all the children who have made my work an exciting and fulfilling part of my life. Thank you to my school principal who supported my efforts and suggested I write this book around the lessons I have presented at school.

Most of all, a heartfelt thank you to my family whose support and encouragement go beyond stating and to my special friends who are always there for me.

About This Book

Children are fascinated with forms of expression and need many opportunities to create visual expressions, as well as to participate in verbal discussions about such expression. By learning about artists and by sharing in their forms of art expression, we gain respect for the individual artists, their time periods in history, and their creative work.

The activities in this book are based on perceptual awareness, art appreciation, and the creation of art in a way that encourages experimentation, self-expression, and creativity, while exploring the basic art skills and concepts. Selected concepts and skills are suggested for the creative activities, however, variations and expansions of the activities are encouraged. Activities can be adjusted for individual levels of skills and development, from preschool through the elementary grades.

Included in this book is a brief look at art history, biographies of the artists, and ready-to-use art activities. All activities involve a combination of language skills, physical skills, thinking skills, and social and emotional skills. Language skills develop through questioning, listening, and discussing. Physical skills focus on manipulation and small motor coordination. Thinking skills include observation, problem solving, prediction, and the understanding of concepts. Social and emotional skills involve identifying feelings, cooperation and flexibility, use of imagination, contributing ideas, and creating.

The lessons in this book are based around master artists and their works. They are intended to:

Integrate the affective (emotional) and cognitive (intellectual) learning processes.
Develop an aesthetic awareness and sensitivity to works of art.
Elucidate art concepts, art elements, and art principles.
Familiarize students with works of art.
Develop a critical sense for the quality or lack of it in a work of art.
Provide art experiences with a variety of materials and techniques.
Allow students to perceive and react like master artists.
Encourage students to express individuality.
Develop an appreciation of art in its various forms, styles, and media.
Allow students to use their strengths and their imaginations, thereby building
   self-esteem.

This book facilitates the learning of different forms and styles of art by recognizing and experiencing the work of great masters. The artists represented in this book include some of the author's personal favorites. They are well known in the field of art and appeal to a wide variety of people. Many of the artworks are widely reproduced on calendars, stationery, postcards, and posters, allowing students easy access to them. It is suggested that utilization of color posters for each artist's work along with reproductions of additional work by the artist would be beneficial in the classroom. Classroom discussions could address how artists used their similar styles throughout their careers or varied their styles over their lifetimes. Reproductions are available through catalog companies or can be purchased through museum gift shops. A list of the artworks included in this book and the museums in which they are located can be found in Appendices D and E. Artists are listed in alphabetical order for organizational purposes, but can be presented in any order, depending on curriculum planning, integration with other subjects, or personal choice.

Lessons are listed by artist and the title describes the activity. The objectives and concepts appear first in order to emphasize the purpose of the lesson. The list of materials is what is recommended for the particular activity described, however, alternate materials are provided for a more open-ended selection. The activities and process section gives the supervisor and the student sequential steps to follow, yet leaves room for personal creativity and individual accomplishments. A few questions are provided to make the discussion meaningful, reinforce concepts, and connect verbal expression with the visual. Allow time to share and discuss the artist's work and then the work of the students. It is important for students to express their ideas and feelings and to appreciate the needs and feelings of others. Discussion provides a good opportunity for the teacher to reinforce the objectives of the lesson by asking pointed questions. There are many areas where art can be integrated into the curriculum. Under each lesson activity, curriculum connections suggest where the particular art activity can be incorporated.

An icon in the upper left-hand corner refers to the skill level for the activity, however, the activity can be modified in order to be appropriate for other levels. A teacher should establish a climate for creative work, provide good motivations, introduce an orderly procedure that ensures a solid foundation, and then allow the children to use their own ideas in developing their work. The teacher should allow the students to work independently until they reach their own stopping points, and then try to stimulate their individual thinking and guide them to attain a new level of achievement.

The lessons in this book allow for children to grow creatively, socially, physically, emotionally, and aesthetically. Creative growth will be seen in the originality of ideas. Social growth will be noted when a child appreciates the needs and feelings of others. Physical growth will be identified through increasing motor control and eye-hand coordination. Emotional growth will be apparent when children are able to identify with their own work and express personal feelings. Aesthetic growth develops with the organization of ideas and feelings through the use of materials. Children grow and develop at different rates, therefore, the lessons in this book are not listed according to chronological age or grade level. They are instead rated as easy, medium, or advanced, according to the developmental stages of the average child. The span in a classroom will vary and it is up to the teacher to explain the objectives in a simple but challenging way. Individualized monitoring of students allows for suggestions and personal assistance. Some experiences that are labeled easy may seem difficult to some children, and some that are labeled advanced could be achieved and enjoyed by younger children. This is where the art of teaching comes in. It is necessary to guide the students in such a way that they will be able to express themselves within the guidelines of the lesson. Remember that the lessons are suggestions and can be modified, simplified, or expanded to create the results that promote self-esteem.

Introduction

To this day artists look to the masters for inspiration. They help us to see the world from different perspectives. Each piece of art is the artist's own personal statement. Choices are made based on mood, experiences, available materials, or simple preference.

Using Art to Create Art encourages exploration, creativity, and self-expression, while developing basic art skills and concepts. The process of creating art allows students to develop visual thinking and creative problem solving, while gaining an understanding of design elements and principles. *Using Art to Create Art* allows students to learn how and why people bring the arts into their lives and how to respond to works of art. They learn to respect opinions that differ from their own and to understand that art carries personal meaning. Students are given the opportunity to explore and control a variety of materials and to discuss and describe works of art. They learn to appreciate the various methods, techniques, and concepts of art.

The art process involves expressing oneself aesthetically; in other words, when making art, artists need to clarify their thinking and convey their point of view, interpretation, feeling, and perception about something in a visual form. Aesthetics encompass the sensitivity to color, line, shape, texture, form, and value, and how these elements are arranged or composed to give a feeling of completeness and unity. To achieve a level of order, principles such as balance, variety, rhythm, contrast, and repetition come into play.

There are different parts to the art process. Artists must have motivation. They need to have something to say about what it is that they are making, creating, or expressing. They need to have feelings and ideas about what they have experienced. Discussing reproductions in the classroom is one way that students gain experiences and inspiration upon which to draw.

Being open to new experiences and a willingness to try new things are important in creating art, as is the confidence to express oneself using a variety of art materials. By relating to particular artists and working in their styles, students gain confidence when they complete a successful creative experience similar to that of a master artist.

In addition to having something to say and the confidence to say it, students must also know what the problem or purpose is that they are trying to express. Students learn about artists, their lives, and their works through teacher-led classroom discussions. Art history in general, and the purpose a particular artist was trying to express, should be introduced so that students can relate to the particular visual perception and, in turn, make their own art expressions. Seeing similarities between the work of famous artists and the students' own work aids greatly in developing confidence and understanding themselves and the field of art.

The art process also encompasses evaluation. Does the work communicate what the artist was trying to say? Is the intended mood or feeling being portrayed? In evaluating art, one must look to see if the work shows aesthetic sensitivity, organization, and knowledge of art. The most basic aspect of aesthetic consideration is whether the work has unity and order.

Artists compose or arrange in different ways. By viewing artworks of different time periods, students notice that a certain type of composition is more prominent in one time period than another. The more they learn about art and art history, the more they gain an understanding of aesthetic principles.

Using reproductions in the classroom encourages and stimulates language development. Conversation is promoted and students develop a greater willingness and ability to express themselves verbally. Children's observation skills increase and they become more aware of the world around them. Concentration and listening skills are strengthened, and vocabulary is increased. Students learn to make decisions in a personal way by exercising their own interpretations. They benefit from exposure to works of art that show different levels and images of reality. Enlightening observations can be brought about through discussions.

There are no magic formulas that one can apply to arrive at a fixed rating of a painting's quality. No two people feel the same way about a particular work of art. Nevertheless there are many factors beyond personal preference that must influence opinions. We must understand the means the artist has used to communicate with us, as well as differences in artistic style and manner of artists' expression.

Most people see a painting as a picture to look at. A painting is a layer of pigments applied to a surface. It is an arrangement of lines, shapes, and colors. It is a projection of the personality of the person who painted it, and a statement of the philosophy of the period of time in which it was created. A painting is a triple experience: visual, emotional, and intellectual. Once we have passed beyond the barrier of the subject matter, our enjoyment of a painting is enhanced by our capacity to respond emotionally and intellectually. Some pictures carry subtle messages. By looking at original or reproduced works of art, we learn about art history and the many varied types of styles.

With knowledge of the history of art, students gain a better understanding of the meaning of art while developing a critical sense for the quality in a work of art. They acquire aesthetic awareness and sensitivity to works of art as they become familiar with many of the master artists.

In this book, lessons based around the master artists involve the use of art concepts, art elements, and art principles. They integrate the affective and cognitive learning process. The emphasis is on the process of finding solutions to the problem presented in the art activity. With personal involvement and sensitivity to the students' creative process, the art educator can guide them to arrive at satisfying solutions.

While viewing art, students should be encouraged to really "see" what is in the reproductions. The teacher's questions should stimulate individual reactions and responses. Students should talk about the artworks, how they make them feel, and what they think the artists were trying to express. They should identify art elements and principles and verbalize their thoughts about the works. Once thus inspired and instructed, the students should then relate the works of art to their own creative experiences.

Art in the Curriculum

An art-based environment allows children to make discoveries, solve problems, and think independently. Art activities can be used in every area of the curriculum to reinforce and extend learning. They capture the students' interest, allow for imagination, and encourage skill growth. Art is a way of communicating nonverbally with others. Art experiences enhance observation, listening, questioning, and describing skills, which are important for language development and writing. Hands-on art experiences make science and math concepts more meaningful. Elements such as cause and effect, light and dark, and shadows and angles provide a connection to math. A wonderful example of math is found in the art of Picasso, whose geometric shapes integrate basic math foundations. Manipulation of materials—sorting and grouping—encourages the development of thinking skills through recognition, comparison, classification, prediction, and task persistence. Learning about artists' lives and the time periods they worked in can easily be expanded to history lessons. Geography can be incorporated when students learn about where the artists lived and worked. Art gives students the common link for cultural literacy.

Children learn more readily when a learning experience is reinforced by similar experiences. Visual and verbal expressions reinforce each other and allow an individual to be more aware, more creative, and more expressive. It is known that learning results from processing stimuli and that stimuli reach the brain through our five senses. Some children learn more readily through one sense over another. Artists, like writers and scientists, are very observant. They try to be aware of what they see, taste, touch, hear, smell, and feel. Appreciation follows focused observation. Students learn to look carefully at the world and to respond to what they observe. They increase perceptual skills by using their eyes to look for the unexpected and by relating to the environment with all the senses.

Children progress through art activities at their own individual pace and should be encouraged to follow their own ideas. These experiences give children an opportunity to express their feelings, strengthen problem-solving skills, and build self-confidence. Art activities are important for physical, social, emotional, intellectual, and creative development. Many visual artists responded to and created with music. Various styles of music can be introduced to students while they create different forms of art.

Benjamin Bloom devised a classification for categorizing the theoretical level of learning skills. According to Bloom's taxonomy, creative activities provide experiences that promote the development and use of high-level thinking skills, which include knowledge, comprehension, application, analysis, synthesis, and evaluation.

The Preschool Child and Beyond

The early childhood years are extremely important in a child's development. Preschool children have begun to explore objects, ideas, and experiences in the world around them. Children's artwork is a way to express their daily awareness. It is important to stimulate young children's minds and to provide basic knowledge and skills that will enhance their learning in the many years to come. Turning everyday interactions into a memorable learning experience is an effective teaching method. Children have a natural curiosity about the world.

Children learn through their senses, so understanding color, shape, and size relationships is important for many learning activities in the very early years. The preschool child should be encouraged to develop confidence in order to function independently and within a group. The establishment of good work habits will help children to become successful, independent learners.

Young children learn by experience, therefore providing them with opportunities for thinking and doing will contribute to their physical and mental development. As with older children, art experiences provide opportunities for preschool children to share meaningful experiences in a supportive environment.

Preschool children should become aware of similarities and differences among the basic art elements. They must be encouraged to explore and experiment with a variety of materials and be allowed to share their creative experiences. As children develop emotionally and intellectually, they will become more aware of their relationship to the world around them. There is no right or wrong in art, only differences; therefore all children, regardless of age or ability, will be able to enjoy and express their experiences through art activities. The activities in this book will encourage children from the preschool years through grade four to observe, question, explore, and engage in art activities that will enhance their natural inquisitiveness.

Children will explore a wide range of materials in imaginative ways. They will be encouraged to use language to communicate feelings, to observe, to recognize, to question, to describe, to think, and to create. The preschool child will begin to experiment with color, line, shape, and texture and begin to compare and find differences. Actual involvement and participation will promote better understanding. Eye-hand coordination will develop and the child will practice following sequential steps. Working together and sharing materials promote cooperation, as does listening, asking questions and verbalizing ideas, which take place during the presentation and share time of the lessons. Manipulating a variety of art media and art tools will enhance fine motor skills.

Children will express their own awareness in their artwork, which allows the process, rather than product, of the lesson to be the important aspect. As children's aesthetic awareness and skill development increases, art lessons can include more detailed work with higher levels of thinking and problem solving. These methods of exploration, experimentation, and discovery are worthy of emulation by teachers who want to successfully encourage children to learn and to appreciate learning in any and all fields.

The Differently Able

In a classroom situation, children will exhibit as many different levels of skill and creative ability as there are children in the room. If there is a child with a particular disability he or she should be considered as just one more child in the room with a different skill level. Everyone's work will be unique because we are all different and each of us creates our own version of how we think things should be. Art is a way of expressing ourselves and we all do that differently. Enjoyment comes from the process of creating, and this method of self-expression builds self-esteem.

For differently-abled children it is extremely important to provide as much sensory enrichment as possible, including visual, verbal, and tactile stimuli. Guide discussions about similarities and differences in materials, styles, and techniques. Verbal and physical prompting, along with models for the students to examine, are very valuable. It might be necessary to adapt some of the techniques of certain lessons to allow a disabled child to participate to the fullest.

One of the keys to teaching exceptional children is the process of breaking tasks down to simple parts. Explain the basics, use demonstrations, and build upon basic skills. Sometimes adaptations of materials are necessary. Special Education teachers can provide valuable information on individual students. It is important to be flexible and to modify instructional strategies to meet the needs of all children.

Developmental Level Guide

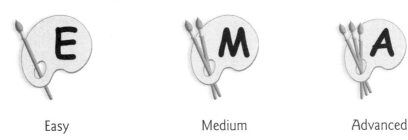

Easy   Medium   Advanced

The lessons in this book were written to be used with preschool children through grade four. Because all children do not reach the same skill level at the same time, the lessons are rated by the experience needed for the particular project chosen. Children with less experience will have more success with the easy lessons, whereas children with more developed skills will be able to explore the advanced lessons, while still enjoying the artistic freedom of the medium and easy levels. With supervision from an adult, lessons can be altered for various skill levels.

Preschoolers need opportunities to become familiar with materials, to experiment, and to discover what effects they can achieve. The lessons in this book can be used with preschoolers if the teacher regards the theme of the lesson as a point of departure and allows for individual personal interpretation. Students should be allowed to make choices and develop their own sense of selection and discrimination. The setup of these lessons is straightforward, yet there is opportunity for individualization. A simple, foolproof activity that allows for personal expression builds self-esteem.

The lessons seem specific in their directives, but students should be encouraged to think independently and explore personal connections. Depending on experience and exposure the students' results will vary. Some medium and advanced lessons can be modified simply by gearing the language of the presentation to a more understandable level for early learners. For example, the Paul Klee Activity 3 is rated as an easy lesson. The experimentation with watercolor paints seems appropriate for preschoolers, but a teacher might question whether a preschooler would be able to use circles, squares, and rectangles to create a head of a man similar to Klee's. After discussing the reproduction and pointing out shapes in the artwork, a game could be played to actively involve the children with finding shapes around the room. Ask children to find something that looks like a circle or a square and bring it back to share with the others. Then ask what is the same or what is different about all the circles, squares, or other shapes. Talk about size and color in their found shapes and put them together to make heads. Look at Klee's work again and see how he put shapes and colors together. Discuss the color of the sun and how it makes us feel warm. Talk about the color of fire and how it is hot. Go around the room and ask children how they are feeling. How could someone tell they were feeling happy? Are they smiling? What might our mouth look like if we were sad? Can they make a sad face by frowning? How does the man in Klee's work look like he feels and why? All this participation is engaging the students in looking at a work of art, associating with the work, getting in touch with their own feelings, and being able to express what they see and feel.

At this point the teacher can demonstrate the procedure of the lesson. While tracing a cardboard circle, the teacher can explain that it is all right if the circle is not perfect; in fact, the teacher could go out of line a few times to show that it just makes everyone's face a little different. The children need not even trace the circle, but could draw it freehand if teachers found tracing too difficult or confining for their students. Tracing is a skill that will develop over time and a little practice can help develop children's fine motor abilities. The teacher can demonstrate adding other shapes to the circle to make it look like the face of Klee's or even the children's own faces. After painting in their outlined heads, discuss how everyone's faces look different yet in some ways might be the same. What happened to the colors when they touched a different color? How does the face look like it's feeling? Was the face someone they know, like Mommy or Daddy? Students can point out different shapes, and even if they cannot remember the names of the shapes they could point out those that look the same, or those that might be bigger or smaller. There are numerous ways to bring lessons down to the independent, exploratory stage of a preschooler.

The easy lessons can accommodate younger preschoolers through simple discussion, visual motivation, play-acting, and demonstration of sample artwork. It is up to the adult to expose youngsters to higher levels of thinking and then allow for individual developmental needs. At this young age a student's manipulation of materials and artistic connections to personal expression are the most valued objectives.

Art History in Brief

The study of art history can be long and complicated, but a brief description will be enough at this time to gain insight into some of the most important schools of art history. First of all, we must understand what a school of art actually is. Artists are often exposed to similar influences during a specific time period. A resulting style of work evolves and these artists are grouped into a particular school of art. Sometimes an artist does not fit into a particular school because his style is so unique, and sometimes an artist's work is so varied that he is in more than one school. Artists are often influenced by other artists, both past and contemporary.

Both European and American art will be outlined in some detail. Eastern or Asian art, which is very different, influenced some of the nineteenth- and twentieth-century artists. Art from China, Japan, Persia, and India often used soft colors and delicate detail. Some Persian and Indian art used bold colors and pigments. They often used ink on silk, paper, or scrolls.

European Art

Cave paintings from the Stone Age (Paleolithic Art) are the first known paintings. Mostly of animals, they seem to convey some kind of hunting narrative and possibly have spiritual meaning. Some are simply outlined in black and some are painted in with bright earth colors.

The next record of paintings was Ancient and Medieval Art, which includes Egyptian Art, and revealed the activities of everyday life. These paintings were found in elaborate tombs.

The Middle Ages began around A.D. 440 and lasted for about a thousand years. Warlike tribes had destroyed the Roman Empire and people found safety living near large churches. The wealthy built castles to protect themselves. Most artists during this time created art for churches and for wealthy nobles. They were regarded as artisans or craftsworkers. Artists often created stitched work called tapestries. These pictures, woven from thread or yarn, often told a story, sometimes about a battle, and were hung on the castle walls. In the Middle Ages the churches kept the arts alive through illustrations of Gospel stories and wall paintings. The paintings were either made on wooden altar pieces or in wet plaster called frescoes. The illustrations were done in books called illuminated manuscripts. Their fancy drawings and designs were made by hand and the words were written with pen and ink. These figures, like the Egyptian work, have no depth and appear flat. Medieval Art usually dates from 3000 B.C. to A.D. 1300. The Middle Ages ended when people began to travel and live in large cities. This was the beginning of the Renaissance period, during which there was a greater interest in science and past cultures.

Traditional Art dates from the beginning of the fourteenth century to 1850. Religious themes were still the basis of art in the early part, but by the end of the fourteenth century in Europe the rebirth called the Renaissance began. A growth in trade, learning, travel, and culture inspired the art. Artists used tempera paints, which were kind of a watercolor that was thickened with egg yolks. The Renaissance began in Florence, Italy, and the artists carefully studied the human anatomy so that they were able to portray it more naturally. Techniques of perspective, which depicted objects at different distances, were mastered. Renaissance artists studied many different subjects and did several different things well. Three well-known artists from this time are Michaelangelo Buonarroti, Leonardo da Vinci, and Raphael Sanzio. The Renaissance artists often used elaborate detail and textures, and light and shadows were important elements in their work. They discovered rules for creating distance and the illusion of space. During the Renaissance the artists sought the ideal of order.

During this time other artists outside of Italy were also creating great works of art. A Flemish painter named Jan van Eyck was the first artist who mixed an oil base, rather than an egg base, with powdered color. This oil paint dried slower than tempera, allowing paints to be mixed right on the canvas. The Northern Renaissance artists painted small detail on their canvases and studied surface textures. Peter Paul Rubens is known for his painting of beautiful skin textures and Albrecht Dürer, a German artist, portrayed exact details like the fur on animals.

In the sixteenth century, El Greco, who lived in Spain, deliberately changed the human figure to make it more dramatic by elongating and twisting it. Another Spanish artist, Velázquez, painted perfect likenesses of his models.

The artwork after the Renaissance in Europe became more varied. From 1600 to 1800, the European work was called Baroque, which means unusual or full of surprises. Many Baroque paintings have graceful swirling curves. During the Baroque period Holland became an important place for art. Many Dutch people were merchants and traders and had money to buy art, so in addition to creating for royalty and churches, artists created for homes and businesses. The Dutch painters of the seventeenth century painted portraits of the middle class and scenes from their everyday life. During this period, Rembrandt was concerned not only with outward appearance, but with the human soul. With his masterful use of lighting, he was able to portray both, in paintings that glowed with light.

In the eighteenth century the French portrayed beautiful maidens more romantically than realistically. They liked soft pastel colors and delicate lines. The British, however, painted the wealthy class dressed lavishly.

Between 1800 and 1900 many different styles of art appeared. Romanticism came about in the nineteenth century and allowed more artistic freedom. Romantic art utilized a wide range of subject matter besides portraits, such as landscapes and mythological scenes. Art in the Romantic style portrays adventures in faraway places or events in nature that are surprising. Romantic paintings appeal first to the emotions or imagination.

By the end of the century, Romanticism was succeeded by Realism, in which everyday life is shown with authenticity. Realist paintings look like something you would actually see. The Realistic painter may modify natural appearances, but will not modify them so much as to distort them.

Another school of art during this time period was the Neoclassic, which abandoned elaborate detail and brought back the clean style of Greek and Roman sculpture.

Modern Art emerged in the latter part of the nineteenth century, beginning in France as a reaction to the demanding realistic representation. These so-called Impressionists moved away from the careful planning of their canvases in their studios and took their work outdoors where they painted a somewhat blurry "impression" of what they saw in front of them. They worked with blotches of color rather than neat outlines, and they were fascinated with the ever-changing natural lighting. Frequently they would paint the same scene at different times of the day. Artists such as Claude Monet, Edgar Degas, and Pierre Auguste Renoir belong to this school of art.

A group of artists called the Postimpressionists felt that Impressionism was too limiting, and developed different styles between 1880 to 1910. They experimented with new ways of painting. Paul Cézanne broke his scenes down into geometric structures, which eventually led the way to Cubism. He used patches of colors in different directions to create illusions of forms. Paul Gauguin used flat bands of color in a primitive style. Toulouse-Lautrec's entertainment scenes had hints of caricature. Georges Seurat and Paul Signac used separate dots of color side by side, a style called Pointillism. Vincent van Gogh painted with thick, swirling strokes and intense colors to show energy and motion and to express his ideas and feelings. Claude Monet, the artist from whom the name "Impressionism" actually came (from his painting titled "Impression: Sunrise"), used dabs of color, either side by side or overlapping, to create a shimmering effect.

Modern Art strengthened in the 1900s when new machines and inventions had a profound impact on society. Abstract Art was a new style in which artists used unusual lines, shapes, or patterns to express their ideas. The first movement in the twentieth century was called Fauvism. The name was given to the group because of its bold wild use of color. (Fauvre means wild beasts.) Henri Matisse is the most important of the Fauvres, achieving harmony in his scenes that often portrayed the joys of life. Another artist in this school is Georges Rouault, whose religious subjects were painted in strong colors separated by black outlines, suggesting stained glass.

From 1907 to about 1920, a group of artists called the Cubists were led by Pablo Picasso and Georges Braque. Cubists portrayed the three dimensions by showing all the sides of an image at the same time. They used geometric blocks, lines, and angles. Color was played down and neutral tones were often used to keep the emphasis on form, often showing the front view and side view at the same time with the other parts overlapping and giving a sense of movement.

Abstract artists gave up painting things that looked real and used lines, colors, and patterns that had no resemblance to anything in nature. The objects pictured lose their identity as objects and exist as pure form. There are two areas of Abstract Art: geometric and nongeometric. Piet Mondrian, a geometric artist, used straight lines, geometric shapes, and patterns. Nongeometric artists such as Wassily Kandinsky, Paul Klee, and Joan Miró were spontaneous and emotional. Their irregular drawings often resembled those of children. These nonobjective artists expressed ideas and feelings by just using lines, colors, and shapes. They did not show any recognizable objects or subjects.

Surrealist artists were influenced by the psychology of Sigmund Freud, often basing their work on dreams, fantasies, visions, and symbols. Real objects were often distorted or put in unreal settings. Salvador Dalí is probably the most well-known Surrealist. Fantasy Art is closely related to Surrealism, with its colorful fairy-tale elements. Marc Chagall is an artist who portrayed dreams or imaginary places.

Expressionism has its roots in artists like El Greco and van Gogh, but solidified as a style in Germany after World War I. Expressionists showed their inner anguish using powerful, violent colors and distortions. Edvard Munch was an artist whose paintings expressed feelings such as joy, sorrow, anger, or fear. Expressionism is often associated with violent, morbid, or sorrowful subjects. In spite of distortion, the objects in an expressionistic painting are usually recognizable. The exaggeration or distortion takes the viewer away from the familiar world into a world of emotion and feeling.

The style of art called Primitive appeared throughout history and was, therefore not a group at a particular time. These artists lacked formal training and often did not use perspective or shadows. Their paintings are direct and sincere. Henri Rousseau, Edward Hicks, and Grandma Moses are Primitive artists whose work exhibits a natural simplicity.

American Art

American art reflected European style, but there was no demand or need for the palace scenes and religious subjects. Basically the Americans painted the middle-class society in everyday scenes.

The earliest paintings were created by the Native Americans, and usually consisted of decorations on pottery, hides, and clothing. They painted designs with earth colors and sometimes depicted animals, birds, and symbols.

Much of the seventeenth- and eighteenth-century American art copied the styles in Europe, because the artists were European settlers, but by the middle of the eighteenth century, American-born artists were developing their own style. Benjamin West, John Singleton Copley, and Gilbert Stuart belong to this group.

The Romantic style gained popularity in the nineteenth century because people sought an escape from their everyday lives. Artists of the Hudson River School, such as Thomas Cole and George Inness, painted realistic landscapes in an idealized manner. However, the Realists—who wanted to paint what was around them and not escape into a perfect dream place—were also prominent in the nineteenth century. Included in this group are Winslow Homer, George Caleb Bingham, and Thomas Eakins. Also in the nineteenth century, artists went west to paint the wilderness and wildlife. A Primitive or Naïve painter of this century is Edward Hicks. In the late nineteenth century, some American artists, including Mary Cassatt, James Whistler, John Singer Sargent, and Childe Hassam, used the Impressionist style that was popular in Paris.

Some twentieth-century Realists are Edward Hopper, Charles Burchfield, Norman Rockwell, and Andrew Wyeth. Around World War II, New York City attracted many Contemporary artists. Although they have little in common, they have been given the names of the New York School and Abstract Expressionists. Artists who concentrated on portraying movement include Stuart Davis, Jackson Pollack, Robert Rauschenberg, Roy Lichtenstein, and Hans Hofmann, to name a few. Some of those who were primarily concerned with geometric designs are Josef Albers, Frank Stella, and Ellsworth Kelly. Some artists who concentrated on color are Mark Rothko, Helen Frankenthaler, and Morris Louis. Pop artist Andy Warhol exemplified another twentieth-century American style in his depictions of everyday objects in a realistic manner. Twentieth-century American art has been overwhelmed with many different styles of painting.

Appreciating Art

The experience of personally visiting a museum cannot be replaced by viewing reproductions. The size of the work, the texture, and the color variations cannot be truly shown in a reproduction. However, studying reproductions can give us insight into the artists' lives, feelings, and views of the world, as well as information on art history.

Every work of art has a story to tell, therefore when you look at a piece of artwork you should try to understand the artist's story. Here are a few questions to help you understand the art you are viewing and identify why you like or dislike the work.

Do we all have to like the same picture? Why or why not?
What makes you like a particular painting?
Does color make a difference in your choice? Why?
What do you think is happening in the picture?
How does the title relate to the work of art?
Does a work of art have to look real like a photograph? Why not?
What are some of the things you recognize in the work?
How do you think the artwork was done?
What kind of lines, shapes, and colors did the artist use?
What feeling or mood seems to be expressed?
What do you think is the message the artist wanted to say?
What is special about the artwork?
Who is the artist?
Why do you think the artist created this work?
What tools did the artist use?
What kind of materials did the artist use?

Romare Bearden

Romare Bearden was born in 1914 in North Carolina but grew up in Harlem, New York. His mother was a journalist and he earned a degree in mathematics at New York University. During the Great Depression of 1930 he was unable to get a job, so he decided to attend art school. He met many black artists and writers. The rhythm of black music and the civil rights struggle were widely used themes in his paintings and collages. Other themes of his art were derived from memories of his family and childhood. Bearden studied art in New York, and after his military service during World War II he studied art and philosophy in Paris. His early works as a painter gave way to the collage style for which he is known. It was in Paris that he learned about making collages. (Collage is a French word meaning to glue or paste.) Bearden liked to add cut-paper shapes and pieces of things with different textures to his work. Some of Bearden's images are typical of the Cubist style. He also had an attraction to Surrealist art with dreamlike scenes.

Collage of a Person

OBJECTIVES/ CONCEPTS:

1. To experiment with and create a collage in Bearden's style.
2. To work with cutting and gluing techniques.
3. To work with facial features and parts of the body.
4. To experiment with using different kinds of paper.

MATERIALS:

9 in. x 12 in. white drawing paper   Sticky dots
Magazines   Scissors
Newspapers   Glue
Construction paper scraps

ALTERNATIVE MATERIALS:

Small buttons, wallpaper, wrapping paper, crepe paper, yarn

ACTIVITIES/PROCESS:

1. View and discuss Romare Bearden's work.
2. Look through magazines and newspapers for pictures of faces. Some faces can be precut for children who might have difficulty cutting, although in Bearden's style of collage, pieces can be cut roughly.
3. Using different papers, cut and arrange the trunk of the body, arms, and legs. Glue down.
4. Glue one of the heads from the magazine or newspaper onto the body.
5. Add dots, buttons, yarn, etc. for detail.

QUESTIONS FOR DISCUSSION:

What did Romare Bearden do that makes his work look a little different? What do you notice about the different papers? How does it look like the person might be feeling? Would it have the same feeling if the materials were all the same?

SHARE TIME/EVALUATION:

_____
_____
_____
_____

CURRICULUM CONNECTION:

Science

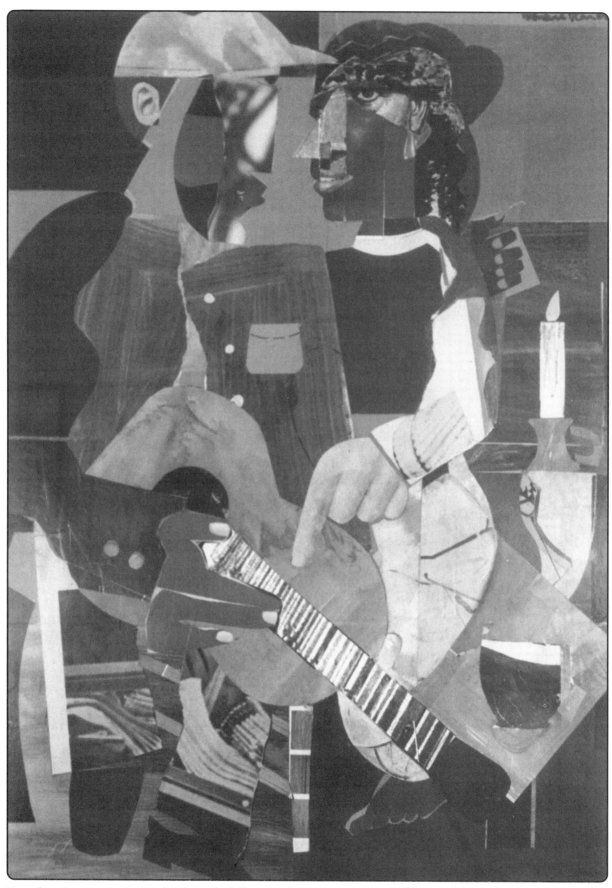

Bearden, Romare. *Serenade.* (1969). Collage and paint on panel, 45¾″ × 32½″. Collection of Madison Art Center. Purchase, through National Endowment for the Arts grant and matching gifts from Madison Art Center members. © Romare Bearden Foundation/Licensed by VAGA, New York, NY.

Romare Bearden

Romare Bearden (1914–1988) lived most of

his life in the Harlem section of New York City.

His early paintings gave way to the collage style

for which he is best known. His collages are

a combination of African symbolism, angular

Cubism, and dreamlike Surrealism. Bearden

often covered up parts of faces with

photographs of other faces in order to give

the subjects different identities.

Neighborhood Collage

OBJECTIVES/ CONCEPTS:

1. To experiment with and create a collage using magazine pictures, cloth, paper, etc.
2. To work with overlapping and layering techniques to create a sense of depth.

MATERIALS:

12 in. x 18 in. white paper	Scissors
Magazines	Glue
Construction paper	Cotton fiber filling
Newspaper	Crayons
Wallpaper	Markers

ALTERNATIVE MATERIALS:

Collage work can include many different types of paper, such as tissue paper, metallic paper, sandpaper and corrugated paper. Old photographs can be cut up and utilized. Yarn and material scraps will offer a textured effect. Add details or areas of color with paint.

ACTIVITIES/PROCESS:

1. View and discuss Romare Bearden's work.
2. Look through magazines and cut out outdoor subjects such as mountains, trees, ponds, fields, etc.
3. Using wallpaper, construction paper, corrugated paper, etc., cut out the shape of a house. Add details such as windows, doors, etc. from magazine pictures.
4. Arrange the pieces to create a neighborhood scene by overlapping and layering.
5. Glue down the different papers.

QUESTIONS FOR DISCUSSION:

What is a collage? What kinds of media do you think the artist used? How does overlapping create space? What do you think the artist was trying to tell us?

SHARE TIME/EVALUATION:

_____

_____

_____

_____

CURRICULUM CONNECTION:

Social Studies and Social Events

Collage of Faces

OBJECTIVES/CONCEPTS:

1. To experiment with and create a collage in Bearden's style.
2. To work with facial features and their proportions.
3. To experience the use of expressions, emotions, and feelings.
4. To work with overlapping and layering techniques.
5. To work with both front and profile views.

MATERIALS:

12 in. x18 in. black construction paper	Crayons
Magazines	Markers
Newspapers (including the comics)	Scissors
Construction paper	Glue
Pencils	

ALTERNATE MATERIALS:

Photographs, photocopies of faces, glue-on eyes

ACTIVITIES/PROCESS:

1. View and discuss Romare Bearden's work.
2. Look through magazines and cut out faces and parts of faces.
3. Arrange faces by overlapping and layering. Add different features or cut some in half in order to add variety to the collage.
4. Make your own faces with markers, crayons, pencils, and construction paper.
5. Cut out letters spelling different words related to the face or expressing emotions, such as sleepy, scared, thinking, etc.
6. Glue down the different parts.

QUESTIONS FOR DISCUSSION:

How can we tell by looking at someone's face how they are feeling? Let's make some different expressions and guess how you are pretending to feel. What is different when we look at someone from the side, compared to how we see them from the front?

SHARE TIME/EVALUATION:

_____
_____
_____
_____

CURRICULUM CONNECTION:

Language Arts, Math, Science

Georges Braque

Georges Braque was born in 1882 in France. Both his father and grandfather were decorator artists and Sunday painters. At seventeen years of age he left school to become a house painter. In 1910 he went to Paris to earn his craftsman diploma and stayed on to go to art school. He began painting landscapes in the pure colors of the Fauvres. In 1907 he was influenced by Cézanne's style based on structure, mass, and form. He reduced nature to "geometric outlines, to cubes" which is where we get the term Cubism. He worked closely with Pablo Picasso from 1909 to 1914; consequently, some of their work is hard to distinguish.

Braque was critically wounded in World War I in 1915 and could not paint for a couple of years due to temporary blindness. When he began painting again he abandoned pure Cubism and developed his own style, which was lucid, intelligent, sensitive, and free. He mixed sand and sawdust with his paint to lend a tactile quality and sometimes even glued patterned paper to his canvas. Braque and his wife lived in Paris until his death in 1963.

Cubist-Style Leaves

OBJECTIVES/ CONCEPTS:

1. To create an abstract drawing based on Cubism.
2. To work with intersecting straight lines to break up the space into interesting shapes.
3. To work with a variety of colors.

MATERIALS:

12 in. x 18 in. white drawing paper
Oil crayons
Pencils
Ruler
Leaves

ALTERNATE MATERIALS:

Markers, crayons, or paints

ACTIVITIES/PROCESS:

1. View and discuss Georges Braque's work.
2. Trace two or three leaves onto the paper.
3. Divide the paper with five or six straight lines in different directions.
4. Color in the shapes that were made by the intersecting lines with different colors.
5. Use a black oil crayon to outline the leaves and to retrace the straight lines.

QUESTIONS FOR DISCUSSION:

What happens when we look at the same object from different angles? Why is it hard to recognize the shape of the leaf once the lines have been added? How are the leaves different from each other? What happens when we color lightly with an oil crayon? When we color darker with the oil crayon? What happens if we put one color on top of another color?

SHARE TIME/EVALUATION:

_____
_____
_____
_____

CURRICULUM CONNECTION:

Science, Math

Braque, Georges. *Man with a Guitar.* (begun summer 1911; completed early 1912). Oil on canvas, 45¾ × 31 × ⅞″ (116.2 × 80.9 cm). The Museum of Modern Art, New York. Acquired through the Lillie P. Bliss Bequest. Photograph © 1998 The Museum of Modern Art, New York.

Georges Braque

Georges Braque (1882–1963) was a French

painter. He, along with Pablo Picasso, founded

the Cubist movement. He used broken planes

and large areas of color. Cubists introduced

collage into their works by actually gluing bits

of details onto their canvases.

Braque, Georges. *La table du musicien.* (1913). Oil on canvas, 65 × 92 cm. Gift Dr. h. c. Raoul La Roche. Oeffentliche Kunstsammlung Basel, Kunstmuseum. Photo by Offentliche Kunstammlung, Basel, Martin Bühler.

21

Still Life

OBJECTIVES/CONCEPTS:

1. To arrange a still-life composition in Georges Braque's style.
2. To experiment with the flat quality of Cubism and break down objects into different parts.
3. To show several points of view of the still life.

MATERIALS:

18 in. x 24 in. colored construction paper
Oil crayons
Objects for still life, including musical instruments

ALTERNATIVE MATERIALS:

Paints, crayons, markers, various papers, scissors, glue

ACTIVITIES/PROCESS:

1. View and discuss George Braque's work.
2. Arrange a still-life composition with overlapping objects. Allow students to hear the sounds the instruments make while they arrange different still lifes.
3. Draw the objects using basic shapes. Add some parts of the objects that might be seen from a different view.
4. Use flat colors to color in the objects.
5. Around the objects, add more bands of color to repeat the shape. This gives a flat three-dimensional look, as if another side was added.

QUESTIONS FOR DISCUSSION:

Where in the reproduction can we see more than one side of an object? How is it represented? Which objects seem to be in front of others and how are they shown? When happens when the outline of a shape is repeated over and over again? How is movement represented?

SHARE TIME/EVALUATION:

_____
_____
_____
_____

CURRICULUM CONNECTION:

Music, Science

ABSTRACT

Alexander Calder

Alexander Calder was born in Pennsylvania in 1898. His mother was a painter and his father and grandfather were sculptors. He had a happy childhood and as a child he enjoyed making things with gadgets and scraps. He collected lots of "treasures" to make his contraptions. He became a mechanical engineer before taking art lessons. He began doing illustrations for the *National Police Gazette* covering prizefights and circuses. In 1926 he moved to Paris and made little toy-like sculptures that became a miniature circus collection. Calder was interested in the three-dimensional aspects of art and when he created his mobiles, space became an important fourth dimension. Calder was the inventor of the mobile. He was also interested in jewelry making. During the time Calder was designing mobiles, he also experimented with free-form drawing and painting. He is best known for his three-dimensional sculptures that are delicately balanced and held together by wires to allow movement from air currents. Artwork in which movement or the impression of movement plays an integral part is called Kinetic Art. Because his mobiles are constantly moving they look different every minute. Calder used this element of chance in his sculptures and it influenced artists that came after him. Calder liked the pure primary colors of red, yellow, and blue. His paintings and sculptures are simple, joyful, and impart a sense of fantasy. Calder died suddenly in 1976 in New York.

Mobile

OBJECTIVES/CONCEPTS:

1. To work with three dimensions and movement to create a mobile.
2. To work with size, shape, and color to create a sense of balance.

MATERIALS:

6 in. x 6 in. colored oak tag
Construction paper scraps
Scissors
Glue
String
Paper punch

ALTERNATE MATERIALS:

A variety of materials can be used to make the hanging parts of the mobile such as felt, paper varieties, or objects of nature. The base of the mobile can be made from sticks, clothes hangers, wire, cardboard tubes, etc.

ACTIVITIES/PROCESS:

1. View and discuss Alexander Calder's work.
2. Cut the oak tag into a circle.
3. Make a coil from the circle by cutting around and around about 1 inch thick. This will be the base to hang objects from.
4. Cut a variety of shapes or objects out of construction paper. They can be theme related, such as ocean or space, or they can be a variety of shapes and colors.
5. Punch holes in the objects and attach string.
6. Decide where on the coil to attach and hang them. Adjust the length of the string for varying heights. Young children will need help tying the strings. Tape could be used to attach the string.

QUESTIONS FOR DISCUSSION:

What makes things move? How can we balance two children on a seesaw if they are different sizes? Why do we have to decorate both sides of flat objects when they are part of a mobile? Why should some strings be longer than others?

SHARE TIME/EVALUATION:

_____
_____
_____
_____

CURRICULUM CONNECTION:

Science, Math

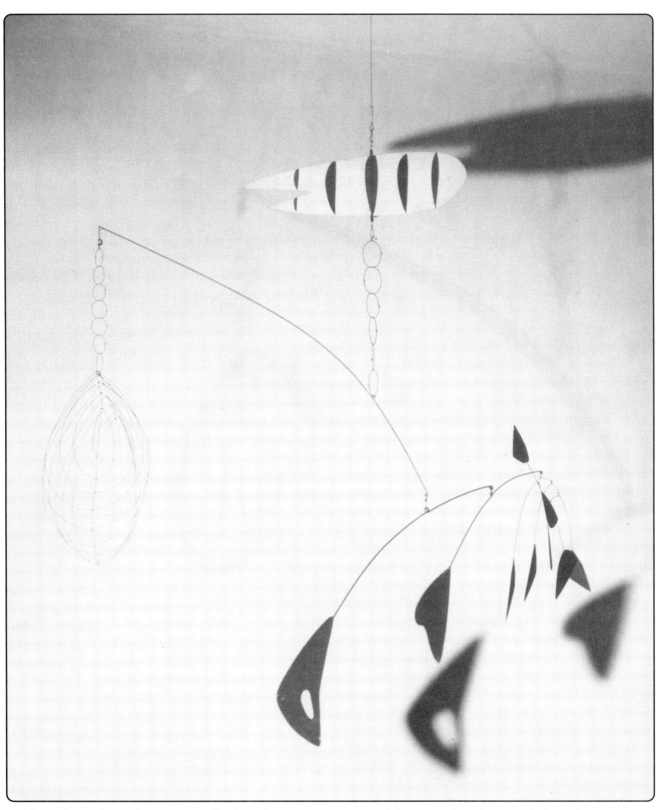

Calder, Alexander. *Lobster Trap and Fish Tail.* (1939). Hanging mobile: painted steel wire and sheet aluminum, about 8′ 6″ h. × 9′ 6″ diameter (260 × 290 cm). The Museum of Modern Art, New York. Commissioned by the Advisory Committee for the stairwell of the Museum. Photograph © 1998 The Museum of Modern Art, New York.

Alexander Calder

Alexander Calder (1898–1976), along with the Futurist group that was inspired by the machine age, tried to capture the sense of movement in his art. Calder became friends with Joan Miró and Piet Mondrian and his work became more abstract. He experimented with free-form drawing and painting, but is best known for inventing the mobile. Calder's sculptures that moved were called "mobiles" and the sculptures that did not move were called "stabiles."

Abstract Faces

OBJECTIVES/ CONCEPTS:

1. To draw an abstract face using line repetition to create movement, as in Calder's *Slanting Red Nose.*
2. To work with facial features and experiment with proportion.

MATERIALS:

12 in. x 18 in. white drawing paper
Markers

ALTERNATE MATERIALS:

Oil crayons, paints, chalk

ACTIVITIES/PROCESS:

1. View and discuss Alexander Calder's work.
2. Draw a face using markers while listening to classical music.
3. Repeat lines around the facial features leaving a small space in between each line. Movement and rhythm will change depending on how closely the lines are repeated.

QUESTIONS FOR DISCUSSION:

What shapes could we use to make the outline of a face? What gives the feeling of movement in the drawing? Why do you think Calder made the nose red in his artwork? Do you think that he gave it a good title? What happens if the lines are close together or farther apart?

SHARE TIME/EVALUATION:

_____
_____
_____
_____

CURRICULUM CONNECTION:

Science, Music

Calder, Alexander. *Slanting Red Nose.* (1969) Gouache on paper, 29½ × 43¼" (74.7 × 109.6 cm). The Museum of Modern Art, New York. Gift of Mr. and Mrs. Klaus G. Pearls. Photograph © 1998 The Museum of Modern Art, New York.

28

Mary Cassatt

Mary Cassatt was born in 1844 in Pennsylvania to a wealthy family but spent most of her life painting in France. She became part of a group of artists called Impressionists because she loved the way they used bright colors. After becoming good friends with an artist named Edgar Degas, who influenced her greatly, Mary Cassatt stopped using dark background colors and painting people in fancy dresses like the other artists of her time. She loved to paint families and children, though she had no children of her own, and she painted people as they really looked in everyday situations. She was able to capture the feelings of love between mothers and their children. Her favorite works depicted women going about their daily lives. Degas suggested that she paint the maternal theme because it had only been done previously in a religious manner; he felt this would give her recognition and perhaps compensate for the hardships she would face being a woman painter. Her pictures always have a warm, inviting feeling, whether she used strong shapes and bright colors or soft pastels. Her scenes elevate the ordinary and intimately involve the viewer. Cassatt used free brush strokes and her compositions pulled the viewer's attention to the main subject. Her subjects are often depicted from unusual angles. To convey the subjects' emotional closeness to each other, Cassatt arranged her figures to overlap or be intertwined. Family members were frequent subjects of her paintings and pastel drawings. Her subjects are viewed up close against a somewhat abstracted background.

Mary Cassatt was very important because she proved that women could become great artists also. She was the only woman who was recognized as an Impressionist painter. Mary Cassatt's work was not very popular in America while she was alive, but in Europe she was regarded as a talented painter. She was just beginning to gain recognition in America when failing eyesight, due to diabetes, forced her to stop painting in 1915. Mary Cassatt died in France at age eighty-two.

Portrait of a Mother and Child

OBJECTIVES/ CONCEPTS:

1. To capture a moment of a child and his/her mother doing something special together.
2. To experiment with chalk pastels.
3. To overlap, intertwine, or somehow show mother and child to create a feeling of togetherness.

MATERIALS:

12 in. x 18 in. white paper
Chalk pastels

ALTERNATE MATERIALS:

Crayons, magazine pictures of women and children

ACTIVITIES/PROCESS:

1. View and discuss Mary Cassatt's work.
2. Talk about special moments you have with your mother such as playing games, reading stories, watching TV, etc.
3. Using chalk pastels, draw a special moment between mother and child. Draw them large enough so that the faces can be seen as portraits.
4. Have background with little detail in order to represent the Impressionist style.

QUESTIONS FOR DISCUSSION:

What do you think is taking place in the reproduction? What things do you like to do with your mother? How do you think the people are feeling in the pictures?

SHARE TIME/EVALUATION:

_____
_____
_____
_____

CURRICULUM CONNECTION:

Language Arts, Social Studies

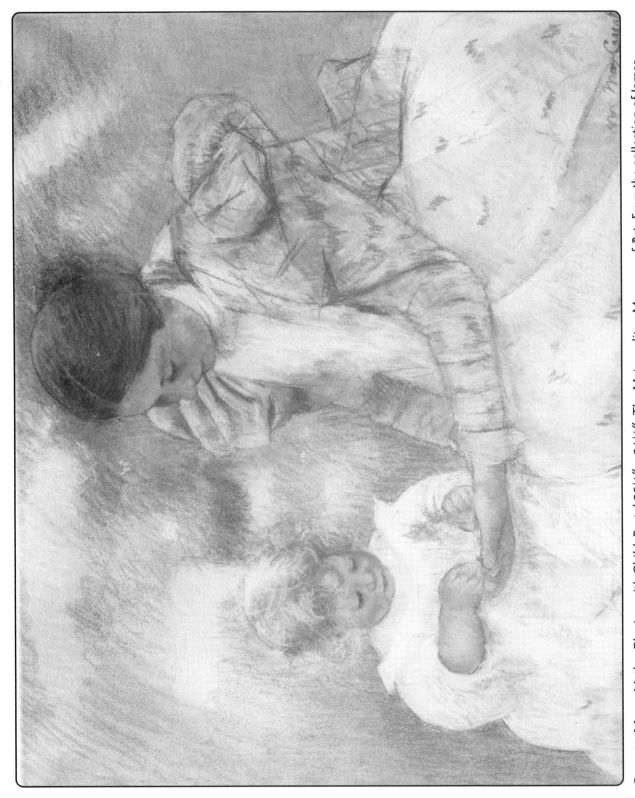

Cassatt, Mary. *Mother Playing with Child.* Pastel 25½″ × 31½″. The Metropolitan Museum of Art. From the collection of James Stillman, Gift of Dr. Ernest G. Stillman, 1922. All rights reserved, The Metropolitan Museum of Art.

Mary Cassatt

Mary Cassatt (1845–1927) was an American,

but is classified as part of the French

Impressionist movement. Many of her works

portray mothers and children in a tender moment.

Cassatt achieved softness in her work, often

through use of pastels as a medium.

Paul Cézanne

Paul Cézanne was born in France in 1839. Cézanne's wealthy father wanted him to work in the bank he owned, but Paul wanted only to paint. Paul Cézanne entered law school, but was determined to become an artist. His father was domineering and did not understand his work, but did pose for some of his drawings and paintings. With support and encouragement from his mother, Cézanne's father finally allowed him to study painting and supported him financially. Cézanne was very moody, shy, and rude, which made him difficult to know. He did marry the first woman he had a relationship with, but they spent more time apart than together. In 1872 Camille Pissaro, a very patient French Impressionist, taught Cézanne the Impressionist techniques and theories. Cézanne used these techniques of intense color and bright effects of sunlight, while emphasizing form and structure. His vision and purpose was different than the Impressionist painters. He felt their work lacked form and structure. He was an intellectual painter looking for ways to create depth and solidity in his subjects. He could show space as well as flat design. He was termed a Postimpressionist; his use of geometric shapes influenced the Cubists' style. He believed that everything was built around three forms: the sphere, the cone, and the cylinder. Cézanne painted landscapes, portraits, and still lifes. He gave strength to simple objects through the use of strong brush strokes, simple forms, and dark outlines. He felt color could give depth, distance, shape, and solidity. Cézanne intentionally made his objects seem unbalanced or asymmetrical. He felt the distortion linked the viewer to the object. Cézanne's use of bold colors influenced the Cubists and the Fauvres. Cézanne began to receive recognition for his work in 1895. In 1906 he died of complications from diabetes.

Still-Life Drawing

OBJECTIVES/CONCEPTS:

1. To create a still-life drawing.
2. To work with geometric shapes and colors to arrange an overlapping composition.
3. To use line and color to resemble a folded piece of fabric.

MATERIALS:

12 in. x 18 in. white drawing paper
Oil crayons
Objects for still life, such as fruits and vegetables, plants, vases, and a piece of material

ALTERNATE MATERIALS:

Markers, chalk

ACTIVITIES/PROCESS:

1. View and discuss Paul Cézanne's work, especially his still lifes.
2. Set up a still life to view.
3. Draw geometric shapes and forms to represent the objects with a black oil crayon.
4. Using a black oil crayon, draw a free-flowing line to represent the material. Add lines to represent folds of fabric and color in.
5. Fill in the shapes and forms with flat colors.
6. Color the table area and the background space.

QUESTIONS FOR DISCUSSION:

What shapes do you notice in the fruits? What is similar and different about the fruits? What do you notice about the color of the fruits? Are all the fruits in a line? Why do you think the artist put the fruits where he did?

SHARE TIME/EVALUATION:

_____
_____
_____
_____

CURRICULUM CONNECTION:

Science, Nutrition, Math

Cezanne, Paul. *Still Life with Apples and Peaches.* (c. 1905). Oil on linen canvas. .812 × 1.006 (32 × 39⅝ in.). Gift of Eugene and Agnes E. Meyer. Photograph © 1999 Board of Trustees. National Gallery of Art, Washington. D.C.

Paul Cézanne

Paul Cézanne (1839–1906) simplified nature into geometrical shapes and planes of bold colors. He modeled objects in a series of planes, with each plane represented by a change of color. For example, an apple would be changed into a roundish object of many planes, which might transform from yellow to orange, orange to red, and red to purple. He felt that geometry was the basis of all form and he distorted form for purposes of structural composition. The objects in his still lifes gained new patterns of planes and volumes through tiltings and flattenings.

Still-Life Painting

OBJECTIVES/ CONCEPTS:

1. To create a still-life painting.
2. To work with geometric shapes and colors to arrange an overlapping composition.
3. To use line and color to resemble a folded piece of fabric.
4. To experiment with painting techniques.

MATERIALS:

12 in. x 18 in. white or manila paper
Tempera paints in primary colors (red, yellow, and blue) and black and white
Paintbrushes
Objects for still lifes, such as fruits and vegetables, plants, vases, and a piece of material

ALTERNATE MATERIALS:

Watercolor paints

ACTIVITIES/PROCESS:

1. View and discuss Paul Cézanne's work, especially his still lifes.
2. Set up a still life to view.
3. Draw geometric shapes and forms to represent the objects with paints and then fill in with flat colors.
4. Paint a free-flowing line to represent the material. Paint in with color. Add lines to represent the folds of the fabric.
5. Paint the table area and the background space.

QUESTIONS FOR DISCUSSION:

Why are red, yellow, and blue called primary colors? What happens if we mix yellow and blue together? How would we make orange? What color do you think should be added to make a color darker? What color to make a color lighter?

SHARE TIME/EVALUATION:

_____
_____
_____
_____

CURRICULUM CONNECTION:

Science, Nutrition, Math

Cut-Paper Still Life

OBJECTIVES/ CONCEPTS:

1. To create a still life using cut paper.
2. To work with colors and geometric shapes to arrange an overlapping composition.
3. To use line and color to resemble a folded piece of fabric.

MATERIALS:

12 in. x 18 in. colored construction paper
Construction paper scraps
Scissors
Glue
Objects for still life, such as fruits and vegetables, plants, vases, and material

ALTERNATE MATERIALS:

Variety of papers, magazine photos of fruit, vegetables, and plants

ACTIVITIES/PROCESS:

1. View and discuss Paul Cézanne's work, especially his still lifes.
2. Set up a still life to view.
3. Cut geometric shapes and forms to represent the objects. Add layered color for highlights and shadows.
4. Layer the shapes onto black paper and glue down, leaving a 1/4-inch border. Cut around the shape to create a black outline.
5. Cut a free-flowing shape to represent the material. Add lines and colored shapes to represent folds of fabric.
6. Arrange the cut-paper still life onto the 12 in. x 18 in. paper and glue down.

QUESTIONS FOR DISCUSSION:

What is a still life? How can we arrange a still life? Allow students to try out different arrangements. How are the colors similar or different in the variety of papers used? Make a connection with the similarities and differences in the colors of the fruit. Why do artists often add a piece of draped material to the still life?

SHARE TIME/EVALUATION:

_____
_____
_____
_____

CURRICULUM CONNECTION:

Science, Nutrition, Math

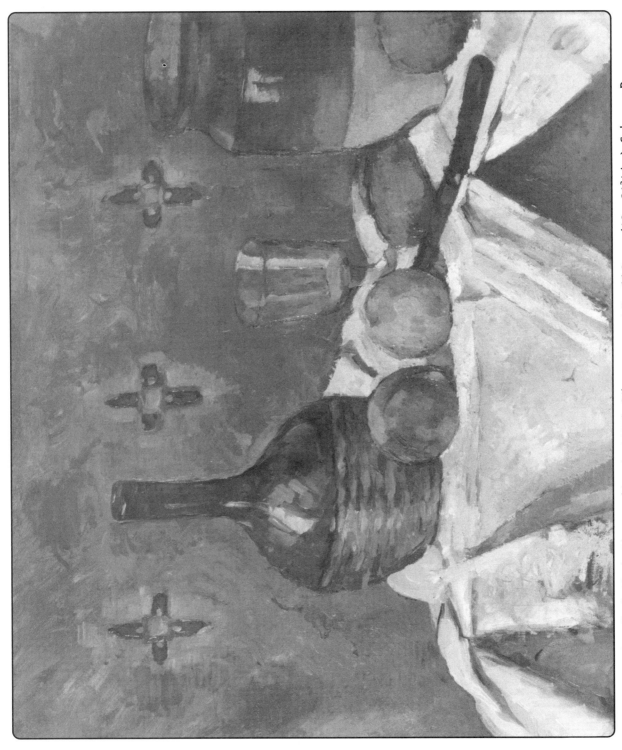

Cezanne, Paul. *Still Life: Flask, Glass, and Jug.* (c. 1877). Oil on canvas, 4.7 × 55.3 cms (18 × 21¾ in.). Solomon R. Guggenheim Museum, New York. Thannhauser Collection. Gift of Justin K. Thannhauser, 1978. Photograph by David Heald © The Solomon R. Guggenheim Foundation, New York.

Marc Chagall

Marc Chagall was born in Russia in 1887. He was the oldest of nine children. His father worked in a herring factory and his mother sold spices and herring out of a small shop in their home. As a child he studied drawing and painting. In 1910 he went to Paris, where he felt he learned more about life and art than from any art teacher or academy. Chagall often painted dreamlike scenes of people floating over rooftops and animal heads with human bodies. Most of the scenes portray visual stories, remembered from his childhood. Some people felt his work was irrational. He often included a young man looking much like himself in his paintings. Many of Chagall's paintings depict someone playing the violin because his favorite uncle was a violinist. In 1915, Chagall married the daughter of a jeweler and she appears in many of his paintings. In addition to paintings Chagall made stage sets, murals, and costumes. He created etchings for illustrations of books and became a printmaker. Most of his works were based on his own life and his memories. Marc Chagall loved the circus and it appeared in several of his paintings. After World War II broke out, Chagall and his family sought refuge in 1941 in the United States. Chagall painted every day until his death of a heart attack, at age ninety-seven.

Images of a Dream

OBJECTIVES/ CONCEPTS:

1. To create a drawing using images from a dream.
2. To overlap images and give the impression of something floating.
3. To work with contour lines as well as solid form.
4. To experiment with crayon-resist technique.

MATERIALS:

12 in. x 18 in. white paper
Crayons
Watercolor paints

ALTERNATE MATERIALS:

Oil crayons, magazine photos, stick-on stars or glitter

ACTIVITIES/PROCESS:

1. View and discuss Marc Chagall's work.
2. Talk about dreams and memories of childhood.
3. Draw scenes and objects from one of your dreams or memories in different areas on the paper using crayons. Some areas should be colored in and some should be left as an outline. Use a variety of different-sized drawings, overlapping and enclosing some.
4. With watercolors fill in the remaining spaces with color. The watercolor washes can be applied directly over the crayon drawings.

QUESTIONS FOR DISCUSSION:

Can you remember your dreams? What about some memories of things that happened when you were younger? What do you think some of the artist's memories were? What things do you think were real and what things do you think were fantasy? Why do you think the artist used such vivid colors?

SHARE TIME/EVALUATION:

_____
_____
_____
_____

CURRICULUM CONNECTION:

Language Arts, Storytelling, Social Studies

Chagall, Marc. *I and the Village.* (1911) Oil on canvas, 6′ 3⅝″ × 59⅝″ (192.1 × 151.4 cm). The Museum of Modern Art, New York. Mrs. Simon Guggenheim Fund. Photograph © 1998 The Museum of Modern Art, New York.

43

Marc Chagall

Marc Chagall (1887–1985) was born in Russia.

His work reflects his happy, fairy-tale manner and

great imagination in vivid colors. He mixed

childhood memories with fantasy. Often his

paintings include people with superhuman

powers, who can fly. His animals sometimes have

human faces and expressions. Chagall also

painted religious and spiritual paintings and

designed many stained-glass windows.

Salvador Dalí

Salvador Dalí was born in Spain in 1904. He studied art history and read the writings of Sigmund Freud on dreams. Dalí explored Cubism, Neoclassicism, and Realism. In 1926, he met Picasso and was later expelled from school because of his difficult behavior. He argued that his teachers were not qualified to judge his work. When he was twenty-four he met the Surrealist artists in Paris. When he was thirty-four he met Sigmund Freud and drew his portrait. Dalí did not lead an ordinary life. At the age of fifty-four, he married a Russian woman who had been his companion for twenty-eight years and was much older than he was. At first they lived in poverty. Dalí had many fears, such as riding in any kind of transportation other than a taxi, exposing his feet, grasshoppers, germs, and evil spirits. Dalí loved publicity and he was constantly trying to shock people. He was very eccentric, and after his wife died he lived his last seven years as a recluse in the castle he had built for her. He died at age eighty-four.

Dalí was a Surrealist who explored the inner reality that goes beyond the rational world of the senses. He was influenced by the psychoanalytic theory of Freud and often used symbols to give his bizarre, dreamlike landscapes a familiar quality.

Out of Sorts

OBJECTIVES/CONCEPTS:

1. To create a picture using real things in unreal situations.
2. To experiment with drawing and collage.

MATERIALS:

12 in. x 18 in. white drawing paper
Magazines
Scissors
Glue
Crayons

ALTERNATE MATERIALS:

Various papers, paints

ACTIVITIES/PROCESS:

1. View and discuss Salvador Dalí's work.
2. Draw a scene or environment with crayons, such as the ocean, desert, circus, etc.
3. Cut pictures from magazines that would not necessarily go with this scene and would make it seem strange.
4. Glue pictures onto the drawing.

QUESTIONS FOR DISCUSSION:

Why do you think the artist's work is different? Can you guess what he was trying to say? Do you think that someone can get a message out by making a picture? Do you have a message about the world that you would like to share? Can you name some differences between reality and fantasy?

SHARE TIME/EVALUATION:

_____

_____

_____

_____

CURRICULUM CONNECTION:

Language Arts, Storytelling, Social Studies

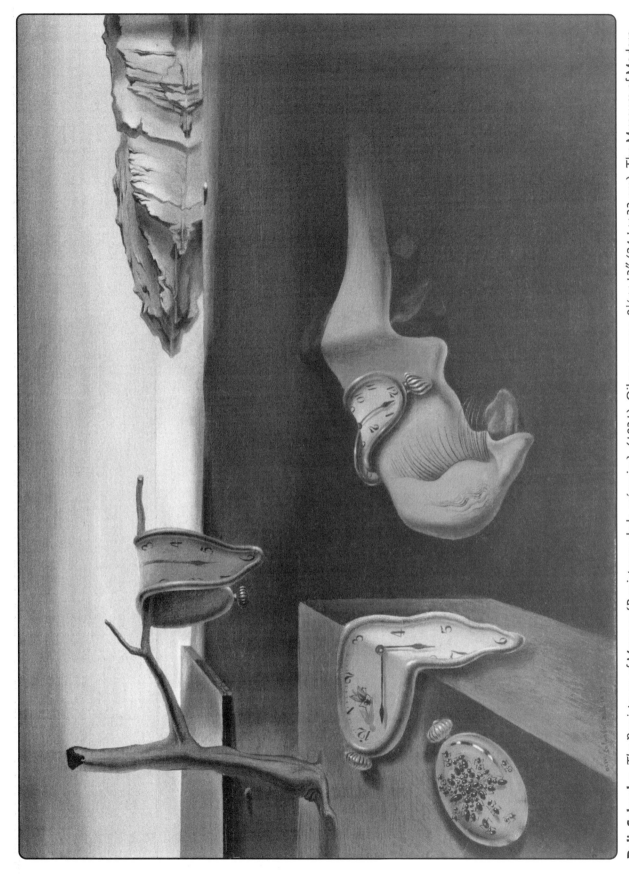

Dali, Salvador. *The Persistence of Memory* {Persistance de la mémoire}. (1931). Oil on canvas, 9½ × 13" (24.1 × 33 cm). The Museum of Modern Art, New York. Given anonymously. Photograph © 1998 The Museum of Modern Art, New York.

Salvador Dalí

Salvador Dalí (1904–1988), a Spanish member of

the Surrealist movement, was quite a showman,

frequently wearing fancy costumes and making

outlandish statements. He pursued the idea of the

absurd and the role of the unconscious in his art.

His sometimes strange subject matter suggests a

nightmarish world. Surrealists used unusual

techniques to link the outside world with dreams

and the subconscious.

Leonardo da Vinci

Leonardo da Vinci was born in 1452 in a town in Italy called Vinci, which he used as his last name. Leonardo had no family of his own, but for twenty-six years a peasant boy who he took in lived with him. He lived during a time called the Renaissance, when people in Europe wanted to fill their buildings with beautiful artwork. Leonardo was not only a great artist but also an architect, scientist, inventor, musician, and mathematician. He used his drawings to help figure out how things would work. The notes on his drawings were always written backwards for privacy. He questioned everything. What he learned about nature and science helped him make his paintings look real. His paintings were much more lifelike than those of any other artist of his time. One of Leonardo da Vinci's most famous paintings is the *Mona Lisa*. No matter where you stand it seems as if she is looking right at you, which makes it seem mysterious.

Leonardo da Vinci used light colors and dark shadows to make his paintings seem three-dimensional. His portraits always had a feeling of movement and his backgrounds seemed real. After painting in Florence, Italy, Leonardo moved to Milan, Italy. He spent the last years of his life in France, where he died in 1519. Only one painting of Leonardo da Vinci's, called *Ginerva de Benci,* is in the United States, in The National Gallery in Washington, D.C. All the others are in museums in Europe.

Invention

OBJECTIVES/ CONCEPTS:

1. To use imagination to create an invention.
2. To use tones and values in pencil drawings.
3. To use detail in drawings and to write a short description at the bottom side of the inventions. This description will be written backwards the way Leonardo did in his notes.

MATERIALS:

12 in. x 18 in. white drawing paper
Pencils

ALTERNATE MATERIALS:

Markers, crayons, colored pencils, charcoal, magazine pictures of different machine parts

ACTIVITIES/CONCEPTS:

1. View and discuss Leonardo da Vinci's work, especially his invention drawings.
2. Using pencil, draw an invention using shading. Add details.
3. Write a short description in the bottom corner making the letters and words backwards as if in mirror image.

QUESTIONS FOR DISCUSSION:

What are inventions? Why do you think people invent? How do we change the tones or values in pencil drawings? What can you do to make something look three-dimensional? If you put different parts of machines together what would you like it to do?

SHARE TIME/EVALUATION:

_____
_____
_____
_____

CURRICULUM CONNECTION:

Science, Language Arts, Descriptive Storytelling

da Vinci, Leonardo. *La Joande.* Musée du Louvre. © PHOTO R.M.N.

Leonardo da Vinci

Leonardo da Vinci (1452–1519), an Italian who was brought up by his grandfather, was always seeking more scientific and theoretical knowledge. His illustrated notebooks are among the most important documents in world history, due to his inventions, ideas, and anticipation of the world to be. His talents were applied not only to architectural and engineering projects, but also to a variety of fields such as natural history, anatomy, biology, astronomy, mathematics, warfare, botany, and more.

Modern *Mona Lisa*

OBJECTIVES/CONCEPTS:

1. To use a photocopy of Leonardo da Vinci's *Mona Lisa*'s face and create a different body and background.
2. To work with patterns and textures to create hair and clothing.
3. To place the modern *Mona Lisa* in a new setting.

MATERIALS:

Photocopy of Mona Lisa's face
12 in. x 18 in. white drawing paper
Pencils
Crayons
Scissors
Glue

ALTERNATE MATERIALS:

Fabric, yarn, colored pencils, oil crayons, pastels, assorted papers

ACTIVITIES/PROCESS:

1. View and discuss Leonardo da Vinci's work, focusing on the *Mona Lisa*.
2. Cut out Mona Lisa's face from photocopy and glue it to the paper.
3. After deciding what the new Mona Lisa will look like and wear, draw the hair and clothing.
4. Add a setting around the body.

QUESTIONS FOR DISCUSSION:

Why do you think Mona Lisa's portrait is so well known? Who do you think she was? Other than in front of an Italian landscape where could she be positioned? People think that her eyes look at them from wherever they are standing . Do you think the same thing?

SHARE TIME/EVALUATION:

_____
_____
_____
_____

CURRICULUM CONNECTION:

Social Studies, Language Arts, Storytelling

Stuart Davis

Stuart Davis was born in 1892 in Pennsylvania. His father was an art editor. Besides learning the tools of the trade, Davis was able to look carefully at the world he lived in. He became part of what was known as the "Ash Can School" where the everyday world was painted as it was seen, with sensitivity and intimacy. At age twenty he worked like his father, doing covers and illustrations for newspapers and magazines. Davis moved to the coast of Massachusetts, where the force and brightness of the light inspired him. His early landscapes were simple, intensely colored, and broadly brushed. Emotional expressiveness came about around 1916–1920 when his brush strokes created expressionistic agitation and his color communicated overtones of feelings. He was influenced by the Fauvres and then the Cubists. To show the relationship of line, color, and plane, he arranged objects in a nonharmonious still life. His paintings of eggbeaters, electrical fans, and so forth are known as "The Eggbeater Series." These paintings became known as abstract, although he never considered himself as an abstract artist. He explored the characteristics of the objects and their relationships with other objects.

Davis and his first wife went to Paris in 1929. She died three years later, and in 1938 he married again and had one son. Jazz was an integral part of his life and he often tried to incorporate rhythm in his paintings. His subjects were contemporary, but he changed them by reducing the elements, exploding them into line, plane, and color. Both his still lifes and his street scenes used the details of commercial imagery, incorporating letters and graphics. Davis died at age seventy-one.

Collage

OBJECTIVES/CONCEPTS:

1. To make a paper collage using geometric and free-form shapes.
2. To use a variety of colors and overlap and layer the shapes.

MATERIALS:

12 in. x 18 in. black paper
Colored construction paper
Scissors
Glue

ALTERNATE MATERIALS:

Paper varieties, paints, crayons, markers

ACTIVITIES/PROCESS:

1. View and discuss Stuart Davis' work.
2. While listening to jazz music, cut out a variety of shapes. Try to have an idea of an object or place in mind and make some of the shapes resemble part of it.
3. Overlap, layer, and arrange the shapes.
4. Words and letters can be added.
5. Glue down.

QUESTIONS FOR DISCUSSION:

Which shapes are on top of other shapes? Do you have a favorite shape in this artwork? Can you find a shape with an open space in it? Do any of the shapes look like something?

SHARE TIME/EVALUATION:

_____
_____
_____
_____

CURRICULUM CONNECTION:

Music, Math

Davis, Stuart. *Semé.* Oil on canvas, 52 × 40 in. The Metropolitan Museum of Art, George A. Hearn Fund, 1953. All rights reserved, The Metropolitan Museum of Art. © Estate of Stuart Davis/Licensed by VAGA, New York, NY.

Stuart Davis

Stuart Davis (1892–1964), an American artist, was first noted for his realistic two-dimensional drawings. Later he became more involved with the technical aspects of painting, while the subject matter was a secondary issue. He moved away from recognizable subjects to compositions focusing on line, color, and shape. His work contains the fragmented shapes that came from the Cubist style, but he also added humor and the rhythm of jazz. He worked with the hue, value, and intensity of colors to allow certain shapes to dance in and out of the picture.

Davis, Stuart. *Landscape with Garage Lights.* (1932). Oil on canvas, 32 × 41⅞ in. Memorial Art Gallery of the University of Rochester; Marion Stratton Gould Fund. © Estate of Stuart Davis/Licensed by VAGA, New York, NY.

Building Collage

OBJECTIVES/CONCEPTS:

1. To create a collage showing a city street and all its buildings.
2. To use a variety of materials, such as colored paper, paint, and markers.
3. To work with color and line.

MATERIALS:

12 in. x 18 in. light blue paper
Construction paper
Tempera paints in primary colors (red, yellow, and blue) and black and white
Paintbrush
Popsicle sticks or corrugated cardboard cut in strips
Scissors
Glue
Markers

ALTERNATE MATERIALS:

Paper varieties, magazines, newspapers

ACTIVITIES/PROCESS:

1. View and discuss Stuart Davis' work.
2. Choose a city street to portray and cut out the buildings from construction paper.
3. Glue down.
4. Add details with paints, paper, or printing techniques. Lines can be printed by painting the edge of the craft stick or cardboard and pressing down.
5. Textures, signs, wires, and other street activities can be included.

QUESTIONS FOR DISCUSSION:

What would you find in a city ? How do the buildings look? What big cities have you visited? What do you remember about them? What did it feel like to be on a street in a big city?

SHARE TIME/EVALUATION:

_____
_____
_____
_____

CURRICULUM CONNECTION:

Social Studies, Math, Architecture, Language Arts

Edgar Degas

Edgar Degas was born to a wealthy family in Paris in 1834. After studying law, he began training in the manner of Ingres, a Romantic painter. Degas learned a great deal through the master's powerful portraits, which seemed to unify physical accuracy and psychological depth. Degas first painted historical subjects, but then became inspired by Gustave Corbet and Eduard Manet. He painted scenes of entertainment in the Impressionist style and became interested in photography. The scenes in his paintings portray dance halls, concerts, cafes, raceways, and theaters, and his work resembles candid photography. He is best known for his paintings of ballet dancers, which he first painted in 1873. From then on he depicted women involved in everyday happenings. He showed the beauty of women in natural poses. His wonderful portraits were often done in soft pastels. He also created small bronze sculptures of dancers and of horses, in which he captured the beauty of movement. Sculpture allowed him to explore many of the same elements as painting while creating a relationship between the three-dimensional form and space. He became interested in the patterns that the movement suggested against the background and experimented with the space between his figures. His compositions are asymmetrical when his subjects are seen from unusual viewpoints. Degas died in Paris at age eighty-three.

A Dancer and Her Shadow

OBJECTIVES/CONCEPTS:

1. To portray the human body in a dancing pose.
2. To work with proportion through figure drawing.
3. To understand the concept of a silhouette.
4. To work with repetition, through the use of a silhouetted shadow.
5. To work with detail, as used in facial features and clothing.

MATERIALS:

9 in. x 12 in. white paper   Pencils
6 in. x 9 in. black paper   Construction paper
6 in. x 9 in. salmon-colored paper   Scissors
Practice sketch paper   Glue

ALTERNATE MATERIALS:

Paper varieties, fabric scraps, lace, ribbon, yarn

ACTIVITIES/PROCESS:

1. View and discuss Edgar Degas' work, especially his dancers.
2. Using a flashlight, make some shadow pictures.
3. Discuss the human body, proportions, joints, etc.
4. With music playing, allow students to take dance positions.
5. Practice sketching the human figure from a model in a dancing pose. Try three or four different poses.
6. Choose one pose and enlarge to 6 or 7 inches tall.
7. Cut out the pose on the salmon-colored and black papers.
8. On the salmon-colored pose, add colored construction paper for details of the face, hair, and clothes.
9. Glue both figures down on the white paper, with the black as the shadow.

QUESTIONS FOR DISCUSSION:

What kind of feeling do you get while viewing the dancers in the artwork? How does the artist show movement in his work? What causes a shadow? Have you ever made shadow pictures with a flashlight? What happens when the light is closer or further away from the object?

SHARE TIME/EVALUATION:

_____
_____
_____
_____

CURRICULUM CONNECTION:

Music, Dance, Science

Degas, Edgar. *Before the Ballet.* (1890/1892). Oil on canvas, .400 × .889 (15¾ × 35). Widener Collection. Photograph © 1999 Board of Trustees, National Gallery of Art, Washington, D.C.

Edgar Degas

Edgar Degas (1834–1917) was a French

Impressionist. His subjects appear quite natural.

Degas painted hundreds of dancers and was

fascinated by human movement. He used soft

brush strokes and delicate color. The movement

of horses was another favorite subject matter.

Dancers in Silhouette

OBJECTIVES/CONCEPTS:

1. To show movement by making figures in dance positions.
2. To understand the meaning of silhouette and use repetition of silhouette figures.
3. To use overlapping to show depth.

MATERIALS:

12 in. x 18 in. black paper
9 in. x 12 in. white scrap paper for sketches
Pencils
Two or three pieces of 6 in. x 9 in. oak tag
Four or five pieces of 6 in. x 9 in. colored paper
Scissors
Glue

ALTERNATE MATERIALS:

Paper varieties, glitter, sparkles

ACTIVITIES/PROCESS:

1. View and discuss Edgar Degas' work, especially his dancers.
2. Discuss the human body, proportions, joints, etc.
3. Allow students to take different dance positions while music is playing.
4. Practice sketching the human figure from a model in a dancing pose. Try three or four different poses.
5. Choose two or three poses to enlarge on the oak tag.
6. Cut them out and trace on a few pieces of colored paper.
7. Arrange the colored silhouettes by overlapping some.
8. Glue down.

QUESTIONS FOR DISCUSSION:

Can you form your body into a dance position? What did the artist do to make it seem as if the dancer is moving? How can we show that the arms or legs of the body are bent? What kind of feeling do you get when you look at the artwork?

SHARE TIME/EVALUATION:

_____
_____
_____
_____

CURRICULUM CONNECTION:

Music, Dance, Science

Three-Dimensional Dancer

OBJECTIVES/CONCEPTS:

1. To create a three-dimensional sculpture of a dancer.
2. To pose a figure, trying to capture a moment of movement.

MATERIALS:

9 in. x 12 in. piece of aluminum foil
Pipe cleaners, one long and two short
Colored tissue paper
Scissors
6 in. x 9 in. black paper
Stapler
Glue

ALTERNATE MATERIALS:

Crepe paper, feathers, glitter, yarn, small block of wood or styrofoam for the base.

ACTIVITIES/PROCESS:

1. View and discuss Edgar Degas' work. Focus in on his dancers and the sculpture *Dancer Putting On Her Stocking.*
2. Form the pipe cleaners to look like a stick figure. Use the long piece to form a round or oval shape at one end for the head. Use one short piece to twist around the long piece for the arms. Use the second short piece for the legs.
3. Cover the pipe cleaners with aluminum foil.
4. Add tissue paper dresses, hair, shoes, etc.
5. Pose body and staple either one or both feet onto the black paper to make it stand up.

QUESTIONS FOR DISCUSSION:

What does three-dimensional mean? What are some ways to show how something flat can become three-dimensional? What are some different poses we can take to show body movement?

SHARE TIME/EVALUATION:

_____
_____
_____
_____

CURRICULUM CONNECTION:

Music, Dance, Science

Degas, Edgar. *Dancer Putting on Her Stocking.* (1900-1910). Bronze sculpture, 17 × 11¼ in. Recently given to the Minneapolis Institute of Arts by the family and friends of Florence Shevlin Tenney. The Minneapolis Institute of Art.

Horses

OBJECTIVES/CONCEPTS:

1. To create a picture of moving horses.
2. To work with proportion.
3. To show distance.
4. To understand and work with silhouettes.

MATERIALS:

12 in. x 18 in. green paper
Two pieces of 9 in. x 12 in. white paper
Black construction paper
Pencils
Scissors
Glue

ALTERNATE MATERIALS:

Paper varieties, yarn

ACTIVITIES/PROCESS:

1. View and discuss Edgar Degas' work, especially his horse pictures.
2. Using pencil on the white paper, draw three or four horse shapes. Make different positions of the horse, either walking or running and in different sizes.
3. Cut out the horse sketches and trace on the black construction paper. The same horse shape can be used more than once.
4. Cut out the black horse silhouettes.
5. Glue down, using the larger horses in front and the smaller ones in back to show distance.

SHARE TIME/EVALUATION:

_____
_____
_____
_____

CURRICULUM CONNECTION:

Science

Degas, Edgar. *The Races.* (before 1873). Wood, .265 × .350 (10½ × 13¾). Widener Collection. Photograph © 1999 Board of Trustees. National Gallery of Art, Washington, D.C.

Albrecht Dürer

Albrecht Dürer was born in Germany in 1471 and was one of eighteen children. He created with many different subjects, such as people, animals, plants, myths, and Bible stories. He used small lines and shapes to create texture, and to express ideas and feelings. Some of Dürer's pictures were carved in wood or metal and then covered with ink, to allow the printing of many copies. He worked with painstaking detail. He used pictures to tell stories. His first works were in the late Gothic period (between the thirteenth and fifteenth centuries), and were characterized by an expressive style of painting, leaning toward realism and interest in detail. Later his works became influenced by the Renaissance period. He learned about the classical technique and style from the Italian Renaissance artists, and they in turn were influenced by his graphics. Albrecht Dürer traveled and studied throughout Europe. He observed like a scientist. Each part of his work is clear and important. Painting the precise details of nature is called Naturalism. Albrecht Dürer died in 1528.

Leaves

OBJECTIVES/CONCEPTS:

1. To observe closely and draw a detailed leaf in a naturalistic style.
2. To experiment with color mixing and blending with colored pencils.

MATERIALS:

9 in. x 12 in. white drawing paper
Pencils
Colored pencils
Leaves

ALTERNATE MATERIALS:

Magnifying glass, colored chalk, charcoal pencils

ACTIVITIES/PROCESS:

1. View and discuss Albrecht Dürer's work.
2. Observe and draw a leaf with pencil.
3. Blend and mix colored pencils to add color and detail.

QUESTIONS FOR DISCUSSION:

Look closely at a leaf and describe what you see. Are all the edges of the leaf the same? Do you see any place where it looks like colors have been blended together? What do you notice about the veins on the leaf?

SHARE TIME/EVALUATION:

_____

_____

_____

_____

CURRICULUM CONNECTION:

Science

Dürer, Albrecht. *Large Piece of Turf.* Graphische Sammulung Albertina, Wien.

Albrecht Dürer

Albrecht Dürer (1471–1528), a German, learned techniques from his goldsmith father that he later applied to his woodcuts and engravings. He had great intellectual perception and a humanistic point of view. Dürer shows fine detail in his work.

ABSTRACT

M.C. Escher

Maurits Cornelis Escher, a Dutch artist, was born in 1898 in the Netherlands. He enjoyed drawing from a young age; his drawing teacher at school encouraged him and taught him how to make linoleum prints. Escher went to an architectural school, but his teacher noticed his talent for the graphic arts and encouraged him to pursue graphic media. The technical skill in his prints attracted mathematicians and psychologists, as well as the general public, as did his use of unusual perspective with everyday objects. His lithographs and woodcuts used realistic details in creating bizarre optical effects. He explored the visual effects that result when different spatial circumstances are depicted on a single plane. He used imagined architectural settings to reflect multiple views of reality. While traveling in Spain and Italy, Escher became fascinated with geometric designs. The Moors decorated floors and walls with multicolored pieces of ceramic, leaving no space between the pieces. Escher did a series of drawings that explored how a surface could be divided into continuous similar shapes without leaving any open spaces. He often used stylized animals, fish, birds, reptiles, or human figures in his designs. Many of Escher's works explore the concept of metamorphosis: the gradual changing of one shape into another. Escher is noted for exploring the mirror image, where the images on one side reflect those on the other.

Tessellations

OBJECTIVES/CONCEPTS:

1. To create a tessellation.
2. To work with both positive and negative shapes.
3. To work with repetition.

MATERIALS:

12 in. x 18 in. white drawing paper
3 in. x 3 in. white paper for the pattern piece
Scissors
Tape
Pencils
Oil crayons

ALTERNATE MATERIALS:

Markers, chalk

ACTIVITIES/PROCESS:

1. View and discuss M. C. Escher's work.
2. Using the 3 x 3 paper, cut a curved or jagged line off the right side of the paper.
3. Slide the part that was cut off over to the left side and tape down.
4. Cut another curved or jagged line off the top edge and slide it to the bottom edge and tape it down.
5. Trace the pattern piece onto the 12 x 18 paper as many times as you can, fitting the tracings close together and filling the paper entirely, even if some of the pattern runs off the edges.
6. Color in the shapes with oil crayons.

QUESTIONS FOR DISCUSSION:

What is a tessellation? Why do you think the pieces fit together? What would happen if a pattern piece got flipped over? How many times would we be able to put the pieces together?

SHARE TIME/EVALUATION:

_____

_____

_____

_____

CURRICULUM CONNECTION:

Math

M. C. Escher

M. C. Escher (1898–1972) was a Dutch artist who experimented with the Mobius strip and with the visual effects that result when different spacial circumstances are depictred in a single plane. A Mobius strip is formed by attaching the ends of a rectangular strip after one end has been given a twist. This results in a one-sided surface that can remain in one piece when split down the middle.

Cut-Paper Tessellations

OBJECTIVES/CONCEPTS:

1. To create a tessellation.
2. To work with both positive and negative shapes.
3. To work with repetition.

MATERIALS:

12 in. x 18 in. white drawing paper
12 in. x 18 in. black paper
3 in. x 3 in. white paper for the pattern piece
Scissors

Tape
Pencils
Glue

ALTERNATE MATERIALS:

Paper varieties

ACTIVITIES/PROCESS:

1. View and discuss M. C. Escher's work.
2. Using the 3 in. x 3 in. white paper, cut a curved or jagged line off the right side of the paper.
3. Slide the part that was cut off over to the left side and tape down.
4. Cut another curved or jagged line off the top edge and slide it to the bottom edge and tape it down.
5. Trace the pattern piece onto the black paper as many times as you can, fitting the tracings close together and filling the paper entirely.
6. Cut out all the pieces of the repeated pattern.
7. Lay them down on the colored paper with the tips touching, both sideways and up and down. This will create a colored pattern in the same shape between the black pieces.
8. Glue down.

QUESTIONS FOR DISCUSSION:

What is a tessellation? Point out a positive shape and a negative shape. Can you make your eyes switch between the positive and the negative shapes?

SHARE TIME/EVALUATION:

_____
_____
_____
_____

CURRICULUM CONNECTION:

Math

Fish Tessellations

OBJECTIVES/CONCEPTS:

1. To create a tessellation.
2. To work with both positive and negative shapes.
3. To work with repetition.

MATERIALS:

12 in. x 18 in. white drawing paper
3 in. x 3 in. white paper for the pattern piece
Scissors
Tape

Pencils
Black crayons
Watercolor paints

ALTERNATE MATERIALS:

Permanent markers, chalk pastels

ACTIVITIES/PROCESS:

1. View and discuss M. C. Escher's work.
2. Using the 3 x 3 inch paper, cut a curved or jagged line off the right side of the paper that makes it look like the tail of a fish.
3. Slide the part that was cut off over to the left side (it will become the head of the fish) and tape down.
4. Cut another curved or jagged line off the top edge, representing a fin, and slide it to the bottom edge and tape down.
5. Trace the pattern piece with a black crayon onto the 12 x 18 inch paper so that it lines up with itself like a puzzle fits together. Fill the entire paper, even if some of the pieces run off the paper.
6. Add eyes and gills with black crayon.
7. Paint the fish in with watercolors, using the same color for each fish.

QUESTIONS FOR DISCUSSION:

What is a tessellation? How are the positive and the negative spaces the same? Would we be able to create other things besides fish? What do we need to be careful of?

SHARE TIME/EVALUATION:

_____

_____

_____

_____

CURRICULUM CONNECTION:

Math, Science

Escher, M. C. *Sky and Water I.* © 1999 Cordon Art B. V. –Baarn-Holland. All rights reserved.

Metamorphosis

OBJECTIVES/PROCESS:

1. To create a picture using metamorphosis.
2. To work with silhouettes.
3. To work with contour edges.

MATERIALS:

6 in. x 24 in. colored construction paper
Five pieces of 4 in. x 6 in. black paper
Scissors
Glue

ALTERNATE MATERIALS:

White paper

ACTIVITIES/PROCESS:

1. View and discuss M. C. Escher's work.
2. Discuss metamorphosis.
3. Using one piece of black paper, cut an egg shape.
4. Using another piece of black paper, cut the shape of a bird.
5. These two shapes will be the first and last shapes in the row.
6. The three other shapes in between will change slightly from one shape to another, resembling the next shape more and more.
7. Position the five progressive shapes, from egg to bird, in a row on the colored paper.
8. Glue down.

QUESTIONS FOR DISCUSSION:

What is metamorphosis? Can you think of anything that changes from one thing into another? When we make a silhouette, what is the most important thing to consider?

SHARE TIME/EVALUATION:

_____
_____
_____
_____

CURRICULUM CONNECTION:

Math, Science

Abby, age 7, **Winslow Homer** Activity 4: *Sunset Ocean Scene with Silhouetted Boats*

Raechel, age 4, **Wassily Kandinsky** Activity 1: *Design Drawing*

Rick, age 9,
Georges Braque
Activity 1: *Cubist-Style
Leaves*

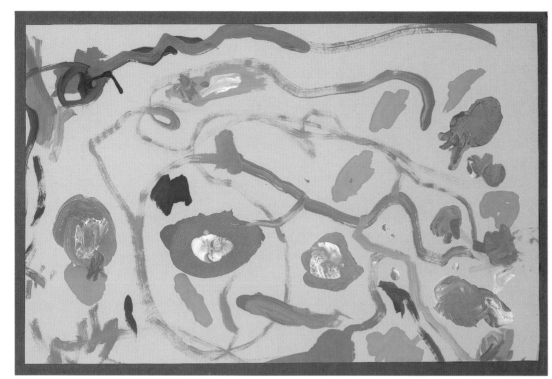

Gabriel, age 3,
Claude Monet Activity 1:
Water Lilies

Linsay, age 4, **Paul Gauguin** Activity 2: *Painted South Sea Landscape*

Raechel, age 4, **Winslow Homer** Activity 2: *Seascape, Alternate Materials*

Sarah, age 5,
Jackson Pollack Activity 1:
Action Painting

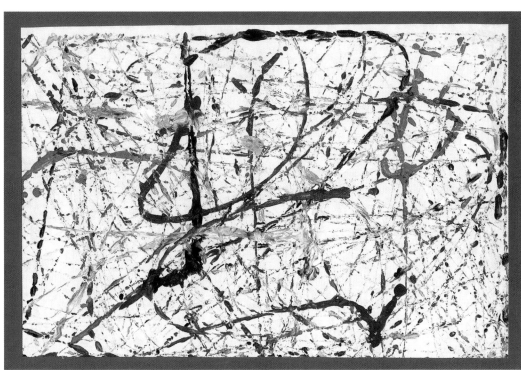

Gabriel, age 3, **Pablo Picasso** Activity 1: *Portrait Drawing*

Andrew, age 5, **Rembrant van Rijn** Activity 1: *Self Portraits*

Linsay, age 4, **Georgia O'Keeffe** Activity 2: *Flower Drawing*

Daniel, age 9,
Joan Miro Activity 1:
Drawing

Kayla, age 7,
**Vincent van
Gogh** Activity 2:
*Starry Night
Crayon Resist*

Joshua, age 9,
Claude Monet Activity 2:
Gardens

Bradley, age 9,
Henri Matisse Activity 1:
Flower Painting

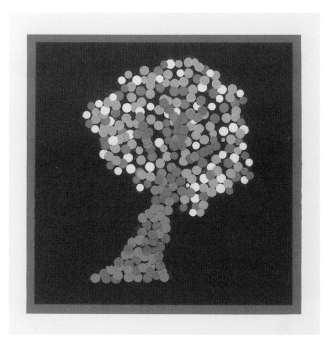

Joseph, age 9,
Georges Seurat Activity 1:
Paper Pointillism

Kyle, age 10,
Paul Cézanne Activity 3:
Cut Paper Still Life

Zachary, age 7, **Jasper Johns** Activity 1: *Collage of Numbers and Letters*

Jonathan, age 7, **Wassily Kandinsky** Activity 2: *Design Painting*

Benjamin, age 4, **Stuart Davis** Activity 1: *Collage*

Bradley, age 9, **Pablo Picasso** Activity 3: *Cut-Paper Portrait*

Hannah, age 5, **Paul Klee** Activity 1: *Take a Line for a Walk*

Brandon, age 13,
Henri Rousseau
Activity 2:
Jungle Scene Collage

Marc, age 10, **Claude Monet** Activity 2: *Gardens, Alternate Materials*

Bradley, age 9, **Vincent van Gogh** Activity 6: *Irises*

Hannah, age 9,
Georgia O'Keeffe Activity 1:
Flower Painting

Paul Gauguin

Paul Gauguin was born in 1848. His mother was a famous writer and his father a journalist. Gauguin's father died when he was very young and he and his mother spent four years in Peru. They moved back to Paris when he was of school age. He later spent many years as a sailor before becoming a stockbroker. It wasn't until after he was married and had five children that he became friendly with artists and began to paint. During a depression in 1883, Gauguin lost his job. After relocating to Denmark for awhile, he returned to France in hopes of becoming a professional artist. He first painted like the Impressionists, but after being influenced by Japanese woodcut art he began to develop his own style. Like van Gogh, Gauguin used color to show emotion in his paintings. In 1888, Gauguin and van Gogh lived and painted together. They both felt that painting should express inner emotions and ideas. Eventually they stopped getting along with each other, and Gauguin decided to leave. Gauguin admired the simple way of life that he had observed on the islands of the South Pacific. In 1891 he settled in Tahiti, where he lived the rest of his life. His paintings reflected the beautiful landscape and the peaceful, natural life of the people. Early primitive artists also influenced him. All his paintings have a quality of calmness, illustrating the contentment he found in his work. They show bands of color and poetic form. His simplified forms, strong linear patterning, and broad areas of bright, flat colors are easily recognized in his native and primitive scenes. The beautiful tropical plants and flowered clothes of the island people inspired Gaugu in. He liked to experiment with color and to use it in a creative way. He painted certain colors next to each other to create a mood.

South Sea Landscape

OBJECTIVES/CONCEPTS:

1. To draw a landscape depicting the peaceful, simple way of life on the islands of the South Seas, in a symbolic rather than realistic way.
2. To use broad areas of strong, flat color in a creative way.
3. To experiment with color mixing and blending.
4. To include at least one islander in flowered clothing. The clothing will be a piece of flowered material glued to the drawing.

MATERIALS:

12 in. x 18 in. white drawing paper
Oil crayons
Pieces of flowered material
Scissors
Glue

ALTERNATE MATERIALS:

Crayons, chalk, flowered wallpaper, flowered wrapping paper, silk or dried flowers

ACTIVITIES/PROCESS:

1. View and discuss Paul Gauguin's work.
2. Look at pictures or travel agency packets about Tahiti, Polynesia, and the South Sea Islands. Locate them on a map.
3. Draw a landscape representing these islands using strong colors in a different way. For example, orange mountains, purple water, etc.
4. Add the foliage of the tropics to the picture.
5. In the picture include at least one island dweller. Cut the flowered material for the clothing and glue it onto the picture.

QUESTIONS FOR DISCUSSION:

Why did the artist use the colors he did? What makes his pictures seem peaceful? Was he concerned about making things look real?

SHARE TIME/EVALUATION:

_____
_____
_____
_____

CURRICULUM CONNECTION:

Social Studies, Science

Gaugin, Paul. *Ta Matete (The Market).* (1892). Oil on canvas, 73 × 91.5 cm. Gift of Dr. h. c. Robert von Hirsch. Oeffentliche Kunstsammlung Basel, Kunstmuseum. Photo by Oeffentliche Kunstsammlung Basel, Martin Bühler.

Paul Gauguin

Paul Gauguin (1848–1903) was a French painter

who settled in Tahiti. He tried to express this

primitive world with imagination and spirituality.

His simplified style of painting was reminiscent

of Primitive Art. He discovered the beauty

of color in the landscape of the South Seas.

His colors are exaggerated and placed in such a

way as to make them seem brighter. Gauguin

was known for changing the actual color of

everyday things to different colors, for decorative

or emotional purposes.

Painted South Sea Landscape

OBJECTIVES/CONCEPTS:

1. To paint a landscape depicting the peaceful, simple way of life on the islands of the South Seas, in a symbolic rather than realistic way.
2. To use broad areas of strong, flat color in a creative way.
3. To experiment with color mixing and blending.

MATERIALS:

12 in. x 18 in. white or manila paper
Tempera paints in primary colors (red, yellow, and blue) and black and white

ALTERNATE MATERIALS:

Watercolor paints

ACTIVITIES/PROCESS:

1. View and discuss Paul Gauguin's work.
2. Look at pictures or travel agency packets about Tahiti, Polynesia, and the South Sea Islands. Locate them on a map.
3. Paint a landscape representing these islands using strong colors in a different way. For example, orange mountains, purple water, etc.
4. Add the foliage of the tropics to the picture.

QUESTIONS FOR DISCUSSION:

Why did the artist use the colors he did? What makes his pictures seem peaceful? Is there anything different about the area that he painted and the area that we live in?

SHARE TIME/EVALUATION:

_____
_____
_____
_____

CURRICULUM CONNECTION:

Social Studies, Science

Winslow Homer

Winslow Homer was born in Boston, Massachusetts, in 1836. His mother, a painter herself, encouraged him to paint. When he was nineteen years old, he worked as an apprentice to a lithographer and became an illustrator for magazines. After taking painting lessons, Homer tried to sell two of his paintings. He said that if they didn't sell he would stop painting. Because his brother didn't want him to become discouraged, he secretly bought the paintings. Homer didn't learn about it for many years later. Although Homer didn't marry or have children, one of his favorite subjects was that of children playing.

In 1873 Homer started working with watercolors, which allowed him to put down quickly his impressions of nature. Winslow Homer liked to spend a lot of time by himself and he often painted solitary figures on his canvases. In 1881, a trip to England became the turning point in his work. He was one of the first Americans to paint outdoors. He learned to capture the sea and he was able to convey the relationship between the sea and the people living near the sea.

At age forty-seven, Homer closed his New York studio and moved to Prout's Neck, Maine, to paint pictures of the sea. His paintings are bold in composition and demonstrate his sense of drama and suspense. They explore light and color and have expressive force. Homer's paintings have a narrative quality, which might reflect his journalist background. Before the nineteenth century, watercolor was used only for preliminary studies, but Homer used the medium for finished work. He liked to paint mystery and danger. He painted fishermen and village people who worked near or on the sea, often portraying them caught in nature's elements. He was a master of creating perspective through his use of muted or grayed colors. Winslow Homer died at Prout's Neck in 1910 at age seventy-four.

Seascape with a Ship or Boat

OBJECTIVES/CONCEPTS:

1. To create a seascape and include a ship or boat.
2. To work with color blending.
3. To try to illustrate some type of weather.
4. To show distance and space.
5. To experiment with watercolor pencils.

MATERIALS:

9 in. x 12 in. white drawing paper
Colored pencils (watercolor type)
Paintbrushes
Water

ALTERNATE MATERIALS:

Chalk, crayons, oil crayons

ACTIVITIES/PROCESS:

1. View and discuss Winslow Homer's work.
2. Using watercolor pencils, draw a ship, fishing boat, sailboat, or other kind of boat. Create a seascape including the boat.
3. Experiment with wetting the paper with a brush and drawing over it with the colored pencils, and also with drawing with the pencils on dry paper and then brushing over it with a wet brush.

QUESTIONS FOR DISCUSSION:

How do we feel when we look at the artwork? What did the artist do to create that feeling? Have you ever been out in a boat on a calm day, or on a day when the water was rough and wavy? What happens if you use the watercolor pencils on a dry area of the paper or a wet area?

SHARE TIME/EVALUATION:

_____

_____

_____

_____

CURRICULUM CONNECTION:

Science

Homer, Winslow. *Breezing Up (A Fair Wind).* (1873-1876). Oil on canvas. .615 × .970 (24⅛ × 38⅛). Gift of the W. L. and May T. Mellon Foundation. Photograph © 1999 Board of Trustees, National Gallery of Art, Washington, D.C.

91

Winslow Homer

Winslow Homer (1836–1910)

is an American painter known for

his seascapes. He often painted

drama and the danger of the elements

in his scenes. He portrayed

his scenes realistically.

Seascape

OBJECTIVES/CONCEPTS:

1. To create a seascape.
2. To work with color, blending light and dark.
3. To experiment with watercolor painting.
4. To work with both wet and dry brush techniques.

MATERIALS:

9 in. x 12 in. watercolor paper
Watercolor paints
White tempera paint

ALTERNATE MATERIALS:

Tempera paints, sponges

ACTIVITIES/PROCESS:

1. View and discuss Winslow Homer's work.
2. Wet paper at the top with a clean brush. Apply colors for the sky and let them blend.
3. Using both wet and dry brushes, create a seascape painting.
4. Add white tempera paint to represent the foam of the water.

QUESTIONS FOR DISCUSSION:

What makes water look calm or rough? What happens if the paper is wet and you add color? What happens if the paper is dry? What do you notice if you use two colors together?

SHARE TIME/EVALUATION:

_____
_____
_____
_____

CURRICULUM CONNECTION:

Science, Social Studies

Ship on the Sea

OBJECTIVES/CONCEPTS:

1. To create a seascape and include a ship or boat.
2. To show distance and space.
3. To create texture through cross-hatching.
4. To work with etching techniques.

MATERIALS:

6 in. x 9 in. black-inked scratch board
Scratch pens
Sketch paper
Pencils

ALTERNATE MATERIALS:

Scratch paper, pointed wooden drawing tool

ACTIVITIES/PROCESS:

1. View and discuss Winslow Homer's work.
2. On sketch paper, draw a tall ship and sketch out ideas for a seascape.
3. Using the scratch pen draw on the scratch board, using the edge and tip to scratch away the black ink, exposing the white board.
4. Using cross-hatching, little lines, swirls, etc., make textures and details.

QUESTIONS FOR DISCUSSION:

How is using scratch board similar to the wood engraving and etching techniques of Winslow Homer? What is the difference if you put little lines close together or farther apart in cross-hatching? How can we create a feeling of three dimensions through cross-hatching?

SHARE TIME/EVALUATION:

_____
_____
_____
_____

CURRICULUM CONNECTION:

Science

Homer, Winslow. *Weatherbeaten.* (1894). Oil on canvas, 28½ × 48⅜″. Portland Museum of Art, Portland, Maine. Bequest of Charles Shipman Payson (1988.55.1). Photo by Benjamin Magro.

Sunset Ocean Scene with Silhouetted Boats

OBJECTIVES/CONCEPTS:

1. To create a sunset ocean picture.
2. To understand and work with silhouettes.
3. To show distance.
4. To experiment with watercolor and salt techniques.
5. To explore wet-on-wet technique by wetting the paper before applying paints.

MATERIALS:

12 in. x 18 in. white paper   Black paper
Watercolor paints   Scissors
Salt (the coarse kind)   Glue

ALTERNATE MATERIALS:

Tempera paints, sponges, various papers

ACTIVITIES/PROCESS:

1. View and discuss Winslow Homer's work.
2. Use wet-on-wet technique to make a sunset sky one-third of the way down (holding the paper vertically).
3. Use wet-on-wet technique to make the water for the ocean on the bottom two-thirds of the paper.
4. Immediately sprinkle the ocean water with salt while the paints are still wet.
5. Cut out three silhouetted sailboats from the black paper, ranging in size from large to small.
6. When the paper is dry, brush off the salt and glue the boats down so that the larger one is in the foreground, the medium is in the middle, and the small is in the background.

QUESTIONS FOR DISCUSSION:

What happens when you put the wet paint on the wet paper? What did you notice about the colors when the paper was wet? How do we make colors lighter or darker when using watercolor paints? What happened when the salt was sprinkled on the wet paper? Why do you think that happened? What does it make it look like? How did you show distance?

SHARE TIME/EVALUATION:

_____
_____
_____
_____

CURRICULUM CONNECTION:

Science

Edward Hopper

Edward Hopper was born in New York in 1882. He was a simple, quiet man who began his career in illustration. He studied painting under artists whose work reflected the realist style. Hopper also made etchings and watercolors. In 1924 he married a painter, who posed for most of the female figures in his work. They lived in New York, but spent summers in New England or traveling in the Southwest. Their travels provided subject matter for many of his paintings. He painted personal portrayals of everyday life in the city. Hopper wanted to show the character of the people. In his everyday scenes he emphasized the solid geometry of architecture and the contrasts of light and shadow. Hopper's paintings frequently reflect the solitude and loneliness in the ordinary life of urban America. His choices of viewpoint were often intended to make viewers feel that they are looking through a window.

Nighttime Café

OBJECTIVES/CONCEPTS:

1. To portray a nighttime café with a feeling of isolation or loneliness.
2. To use shadows.
3. To experiment with cut-paper techniques.

MATERIALS:

12 in. x 18 in. dark blue paper
Construction paper
Scissors
Glue
Magazine
Flashlight

ALTERNATE MATERIALS:

Paper varieties, chalk

ACTIVITIES/PROCESS:

1. View and discuss Edward Hopper's work.
2. Talk about a nighttime neighborhood scene where few people are around.
3. Experience making some shadows of objects using a flashlight.
4. Using construction paper, cut out a scene. Use black paper for shadows.
5. Cut out a person or two from a magazine to include in the scene.

QUESTIONS FOR DISCUSSION:

How did Edward Hopper make his scenes seem lonely? What makes you feel lonely? Why do you think he made it seem that way? How do we know that it is nighttime? What makes a shadow and when would we see one?

SHARE TIME/EVALUATION:

_____
_____
_____
_____

CURRICULUM CONNECTION:

Social Studies, Science, Language Arts

Hopper, Edward. American, 1882-1967. *Nighthawks.* (1942). Oil on canvas, 84.1 × 152.4 cm. Friends of American Art Collection, 1942.51. Photograph © 1998, The Art Institute of Chicago. All rights reserved.

Edward Hopper

Edward Hopper (1882–1967), who was born in

New York, often painted realistic, lonely scenes in

America with a touch of romanticism. His people

are anonymous and usually withdrawn. The

stillness of his scenes is often cold and

uninviting. Hopper worked with strong lights and

shadows and his work emphasizes the isolation

and separateness of people in the everyday world.

Jasper Johns

Jasper Johns was born in South Carolina in 1930. He studied art at the University of South Carolina. Johns moved to New York in 1952 and began painting seriously. Abstract Expressionism was popular at this time. Johns' friends, who were artists, musicians, and dancers, encouraged him to make art that expressed his ideas and a particular point of view. Jasper Johns decided to focus on familiar objects like numbers, maps, and flags, to help engage the viewer in his work. Johns enjoyed painting with encaustics, which are pigments mixed with melted beeswax and resin. After they are painted on the canvas, they are heated. Other artists were influenced by Johns' work and a new form of art using everyday objects, called Pop Art, emerged.

Collage of Numbers and Letters

OBJECTIVES/CONCEPTS:

1. To design a collage using numbers and letters.
2. To experiment with printing techniques and the reverse or mirror image.
3. To experiment with painting techniques.
4. To work with a variety of sizes, thicknesses, and colors.
5. To experiment with overlapping.

MATERIALS:

12 in. x 18 in. white drawing paper
Tempera paints
Trays for paints
Paintbrushes

Numbers and letters for printing
   (sponge, Styrofoam, rubber stamp)
Construction paper numbers and letters

ALTERNATE MATERIALS:

Watercolor paints, oil crayons, number stickers

ACTIVITIES/PROCESS:

1. View and discuss Jasper Johns' work.
2. Discuss printing techniques and mirror images.
3. Use a variety of colors, sizes, and kinds of numbers and letters.
4. Dip letters or numbers into the tray filled with a small amount of paint. Wipe off excess paint.
5. Press on the white paper and lift. This can be done more than one time.
6. Fill paper with a variety of repeated prints.
7. For rubber stamps use inkpad.
8. Paint a few letters and numbers with a brush.
9. Glue down a few construction paper numbers or letters.

QUESTIONS FOR DISCUSSION:

Are there any numbers that are the same? What is different about the letters and or numbers? Are there any numbers or letters that are on top of another one? What do you notice about the different kinds of materials that you used?

SHARE TIME/EVALUATION:

_____
_____
_____
_____

CURRICULUM CONNECTION:

Math

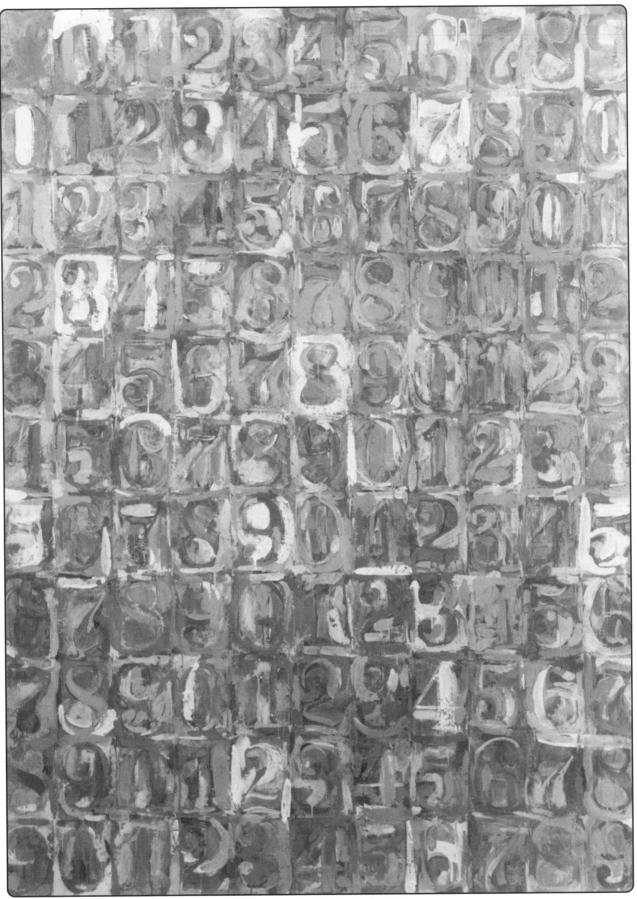

Johns, Jasper. *Numbers in Color.* (1958-59). Encaustic and newspaper on canvas, 66½ × 49½″. Albright Knox Art Gallery, Buffalo, New York. Gift of Seymour H. Knox, 1959. © Jasper Johns/Licensed by VAGA, New York, NY.

Jasper Johns

Jasper Johns (1930–) was born in South Carolina.

In his art, he encouraged people to see familiar

things in new ways. His use of everyday subjects

like numbers, maps, and flags was intended to

engage the viewer in his work. Johns also is a

printmaker and sculptor. Johns was influential to

the artists of the Pop Art style.

Number Design

OBJECTIVES/CONCEPTS:

1. To make a number design using block numbers.
2. To use a checkerboard setup, by putting the numbers in boxes.
3. To work with organic shapes and a variety of colors.

MATERIALS:

9 in. x 12 in. white drawing paper
Pencils
Colored markers

ALTERNATE MATERIALS:

Colored pencils, crayons, chalk, oil crayons

ACTIVITIES/PROCESS:

1. View and discuss Jasper Johns' work.
2. Divide paper into twelve equal squares.
3. With pencil make block numbers in the squares in any order. Make them large enough to fill the squares.
4. Use colored markers to color in some of the numbers.
5. Make free-flowing lines and organic shapes to fill the space around the numbers.
6. Color in the shapes.

QUESTIONS FOR DISCUSSION:

What kind of patterns can you find? Which is your favorite? What kinds of shapes can you find in the negative areas?

SHARE TIME/EVALUATION:

_____

_____

_____

_____

CURRICULUM CONNECTION:

Math

The American Flag

OBJECTIVES/CONCEPTS:

1. To paint three flags superimposed on top of each other using different size lines.
2. To experiment with painting techniques.
3. To create the illusion of depth.

MATERIALS:

12 in. x 18 in. white drawing paper
Ruler
Pencils
Tempera paints (red, white, blue, and black)
Paintbrush
Star stencils in three sizes

ALTERNATE MATERIALS:

Watercolor paints, three blue rectangles of paper in different sizes, red and white strips of paper in different thicknesses

ACTIVITIES/PROCESS:

1. View and discuss Jasper Johns' work, focusing on *Three Flags*.
2. Draw a rectangle in the middle of the paper.
3. Draw a larger rectangle around it, halfway between the edge of the paper and the first rectangle.
4. Make each rectangle into a flag, drawing the lines a little wider with each flag. The stars will also increase in size proportionately to the flag size.
5. Paint in.

QUESTIONS FOR DISCUSSION:

As the flags get larger, what seems to happen? How do the colors vary? Why does it seem like the flags are moving toward or away from us?

SHARE TIME/EVALUATION:

_____
_____
_____
_____

CURRICULUM CONNECTION:

Social Studies, Science

Johns, Jasper. *Three Flags.* (1958). Encaustic on canvas. 30⅞ × 45½ × 5 in. (78.4 × 115.6 × 12.7 cm.) 50th Anniversary Gift of the Gilman Foundation, Inc., The Lauder Foundation, A. Alfred Taubman, an anonymous donor, and purchase. Collection of Whitney Museum of American Art, New York. Photograph Copyright © 1999 Whitney Museum of American Art. © Jasper Johns/Licensed by VAGA, New York, NY.

Wassily Kandinsky

Wassily Kandinsky was born in Moscow in 1866. He was an originator of Abstract Art. In 1921 he helped found the Academy of Arts and Sciences, but the following year he went to work at the Bauhaus in Germany, which is an influential school experimenting with Abstract and Modern Art. During his Bauhaus period from 1922 to 1932, he concentrated on theme of the circle, square, and triangle. Kandinsky was also a musician and examined the parallels between art and music. Kandinsky felt that music and abstract visual forms and colors could suggest feelings and ideas in a similar way. Kandinsky used an event or story to create a painting. He left clues to suggest an idea and with colors and forms he expressed the nature of the action. Kandinsky studied the ways in which colors and forms work together. He related colors to sounds, tastes, movements, feelings, and emotions. He used color and form to liberate the painter from the object and he created abstractions of reality. In his paintings, colors take on independent meaning and become forms to represent the subject matter. From 1910 to 1914, he painted a series of abstract "Impressions," "Improvisions," and "Compositions," which were based on his observations of nature and impressions of the world. The "Improvisions" came from a sudden impulse and the unconscious mind, whereas the "Impressions" are more representational and the "Compositions" are more studied. Kandinsky died in 1944.

Design Drawing

OBJECTIVES/CONCEPTS:

1. To work with a variety of lines (fat, thin, straight, curved, zigzag).
2. To work with a variety of colors and color blending.
3. To use imagination to create an abstract drawing.
4. To experiment with oil crayons as a medium.

MATERIALS:

12 in. x 18 in. white drawing paper
Oil crayons

ALTERNATE MATERIALS:

Chalk, markers

ACTIVITIES/PROCESS:

1. View and discuss some of Wassily Kandinsky's work.
2. Use a black oil crayon to draw a variety of lines onto the paper. Limit the use of lines to six or seven. Some of the lines should overlap each other. Suggest using some free-flowing lines as well as straight and zigzag.
3. Fill in all the space on the paper with a variety of colors. Make the color areas blend into each other. Discuss design techniques.
4. Retrace the black lines to make them stand out from the colored background.

QUESTIONS FOR DISCUSSION:

What kinds of lines do you see? Can you find some shapes? Where are there two colors mixed together? How many lines can you find? Are there any places where the same color was used again in another place?

SHARE TIME/EVALUATION:

_____
_____
_____
_____

CURRICULUM CONNECTION:

Math

Kandinsky, Wassily. *Improvisation 31 (Sea Battle).* (1913). Canvas//oil on linen, 1.451 × 1.197 (55⅜ × 47⅛).
Ailsa Mellon Bruce Fund. Photograph © 1999 Board of Trustees, National Gallery of Art, Washington, D.C.

Wassily Kandinsky

Russian-born Wassily Kandinsky

(1866–1944) was one of the twentieth

century's major abstract artists. He created

with vibrant colors, geometric forms,

and powerful movement.

Design Painting

OBJECTIVES/CONCEPTS:

1. To work with a variety of lines (fat, thin, straight, curved, zigzag).
2. To work with a variety of colors and color blending.
3. To use imagination to create an abstract drawing.
4. To experiment with watercolor paints as a medium.

MATERIALS:

12 in. x 18 in. white drawing paper
Watercolor paints

ALTERNATE MATERIALS:

Tempera paint

ACTIVITIES/PROCESS:

1. View and discuss Wassily Kandinsky's work.
2. Discuss design techniques and abstract work. Have music on while the children work.
3. Using watercolor paints, create a design by using shapes and lines.
4. Pull the design together by painting black lines throughout the composition. Overlap and repeat some lines and shapes.

QUESTIONS FOR DISCUSSION:

What kinds of lines do you see? Can you find some shapes? What makes some colors darker than others? What happens when two colors mix together? What happens if you have a lot of water on your brush? Did the music make you paint a certain way?

SHARE TIME/EVALUATION:

_____
_____
_____
_____

CURRICULUM CONNECTION:

Music, Math

Geometric Design

OBJECTIVES/CONCEPTS:

1. To work with a variety of lines (fat, thin, straight, curved, zigzag).
2. To work with a variety of colors and color blending.
3. To use imagination to create an abstract drawing.
4. To overlap lines and shapes.
5. To use a variety of repeated shapes.
6. To experiment with watercolor paints as a medium.

MATERIALS:

9 in. x 12 in. white drawing paper
Ruler
Colored pencils

Compass
Stenciled shapes
Watercolor paints

ALTERNATE MATERIALS:

Permanent markers, crayons, chalk

ACTIVITIES/PROCESS:

1. View and discuss some of Wassily Kandinsky's work.
2. Using colored pencils, ruler, compass, and stenciled shapes, draw a variety of lines and shapes that overlap and connect.
3. Color in shapes with colored pencils or leave some to be filled in with watercolor paints.
4. Using watercolor paints, fill in all the white spaces with a variety of colors and blended colors.

QUESTIONS FOR DISCUSSION:

What kinds of lines can you find? What shapes? Where are the overlapping areas? Do any lines intersect? What makes the design seem balanced? Can you note the differences between the materials used?

SHARE TIME/EVALUATION:

_____

_____

_____

_____

CURRICULUM CONNECTION:

Math

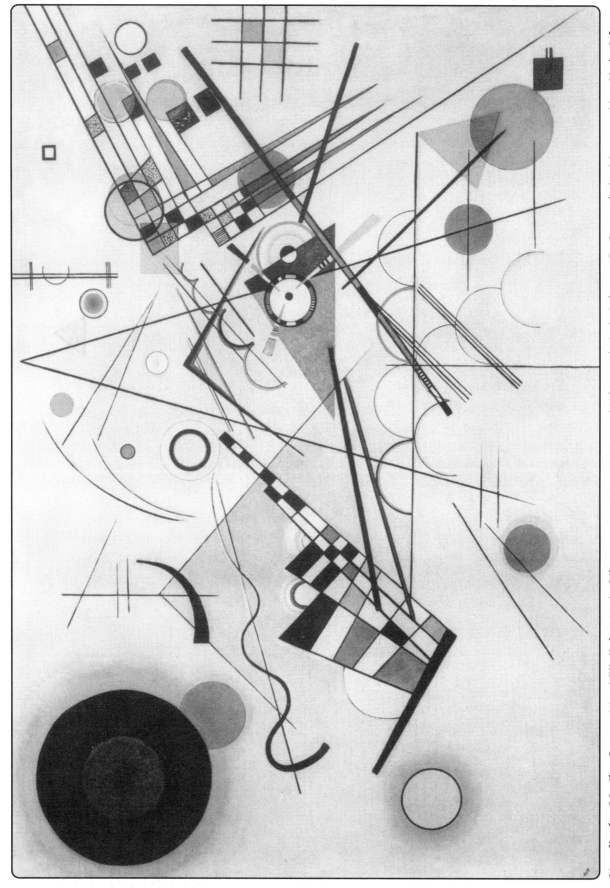

Kandinsky, Vasily. *Composition VIII.* (July 1923). Oil on canvas. 140 × 200 cms (55⅛ × 79⅛ in.). Solomon R. Guggenheim Museum, New York. Gift, Solomon R. Guggenheim, 1937. Photograph by Robert E. Mates © The Solomon R. Guggenheim Foundation, New York.

Checkerboard Design

OBJECTIVES/CONCEPTS:

1. To use straight lines to create overlapping checkerboard patterns.
2. To use color to create patterns in a checkerboard design.
3. To arrange overlapped shapes as part of the abstract design.

MATERIALS:

9 in. x 12 in. white drawing paper
Ruler
Pencils
Crayons

ALTERNATE MATERIALS:

Markers, colored pencils

ACTIVITIES/PROCESS:

1. View and discuss some of Wassily Kandinsky's work.
2. Using a pencil and ruler, draw overlapping squares and triangles.
3. A layered effect can be used, where shapes get larger as they surround each other.
4. Divide the shapes into checkerboard patterns.
5. Color the checkerboard squares differently in each shape.

QUESTIONS FOR DISCUSSION:

What creates the feeling of overlapping? What are some patterns? What do you notice about color choices?
What shapes can you find?

SHARE TIME/EVALUATION:

_____
_____
_____
_____

CURRICULUM CONNECTION:

Math

Paul Klee

Paul Klee was born in Switzerland in 1879. His mother was an amateur painter and his father a music teacher. Klee played the violin in a symphony orchestra but he enjoyed art more. In his early years he drew and painted many whimsical pictures from his imagination. In 1914 he took a trip down the Nile River in North Africa. He experienced the magic of color through the effects of the bright sunlight; he felt this land had a fairy-tale quality. He studied the artwork of African tribes, as well as art made by children, because he felt that simple shapes and forms best expressed ideas and feelings. Most of Paul Klee's paintings are small and imaginative.

Klee was aware of a group of contemporary artists, called Futurists, who believed that all the newly invented machinery could make a manmade world better than the natural one. Klee did a watercolor and pen-and-ink picture called *Twittering Machine,* which mocked the Futurist point of view. Klee did not feel machines could make anything as beautiful as nature. In the painting the birds are not realistic and thus suggest that their song would not sound natural either.

Take a Line for a Walk

OBJECTIVES/CONCEPTS:

1. To use a variety of lines.
2. To find shapes within the intersected lines and color them in.
3. To create this design from an imaginary walk.

MATERIALS:

Black markers
Crayons

ALTERNATE MATERIALS:

Colored chalk, oil crayons

ACTIVITIES/PROCESS:

1. View and discuss Paul Klee's work.
2. With a black marker draw a line as you describe a walk, going around something, sliding down or climbing up, going in or out, etc.
3. Find shapes that have been made and color them in with crayons.

QUESTIONS FOR DISCUSSION:

What kinds of lines can you find? Can you find the same shape more than once? What kinds of lines make what kinds of shapes? Find and name some colors. By looking at the artwork, can you guess what part of your walk you might have been on?

SHARE TIME/EVALUATION:

_____
_____
_____
_____

CURRICULUM CONNECTION:

Language Arts, Math

Klee, Paul. *Twittering Machine* {Zwitscher-Maschine} . (1922). Watercolor, and pen and ink on oil transfer drawing on paper, mounted on cardboard, 25¼ × 19″ (63.8 × 48.1 cm). The Museum of Modern Art, New York. Purchase. Photograph © 1998 The Museum of Modern Art, New York.

Paul Klee

Paul Klee (1879–1940), who was born in

Switzerland, once wrote, "Art does not reproduce

what we see. It makes us see." Klee uses simple

geometric forms and arranges them in a childlike

manner. His imaginative drawings of doodles

seem as if the artist was, in Klee's own words,

"taking a line for a walk."

Klee's Twittering Machine

OBJECTIVES/CONCEPTS:

1. To create a machine, using a variety of simple lines and shapes.
2. To make images of birds singing.
3. To experiment with watercolor techniques.

MATERIALS:

12 in. x 18 in. white drawing paper
Pencils
Watercolor paints
Fine-line black markers

ALTERNATE MATERIALS:

Markers, crayons, chalk

ACTIVITIES/PROCESS:

1. View and discuss Paul Klee's work, focusing on his work called *Twittering Machine*.
2. Draw with pencil some kind of a machine that would make the song of birds. Add simple shapes and lines to make birdlike figures.
3. Paint in with watercolors.
4. Go over the pencil lines with the black marker.

QUESTIONS FOR DISCUSSION:

Can you name some different kinds of lines that the artist used in his work? This artwork is about a machine. How can we tell it is a machine? What makes it look like something is happening in the picture? What kind of machine would you like to make and why?

SHARE TIME/EVALUATION:

_____
_____
_____
_____

CURRICULUM CONNECTION:

Social Studies, Language Arts, Science

Head of a Man

OBJECTIVES/CONCEPTS:

1. To create the head of a man like that in Paul Klee's painting.
2. To use flat geometric shapes and a blend of colors.
3. To work with warm colors.
4. To experiment with watercolor techniques.

MATERIALS:

12 in. x 18 in. white paper
Pencils
Large circle to trace
Watercolor paints

ALTERNATE MATERIALS:

Tempera paints, chalk, crayons

ACTIVITIES/PROCESS:

1. View and discuss Paul Klee's work, focusing on *Senecio* ("Head of a Man").
2. Trace the circle with pencil.
3. Add a square neck, shoulders, and facial details.
4. Divide these shapes into small rectangles and squares.
5. Paint in with watercolors, similar to the warm style of Klee's.

QUESTIONS FOR DISCUSSION:

What do you notice about this work? Why don't you think the artist made him look real? What shapes can you find? Do you think he used certain colors for a special reason?

SHARE TIME/EVALUATION:

_____

_____

_____

_____

CURRICULUM CONNECTION:

Language Arts, Math, Science

Klee, Paul. *Senecio.* (1922). Oil on gauze on cardboard, 40.5 × 38 cm. Oeffentliche Kunstsammlung Basel, Kunstmuseum. Photo by Oeffentliche Kunstsammlung Basel, Martin Bühler.

Henri Matisse

Henri Matisse was born in 1869 in France. His father was a grain merchant. At eighteen he studied law in Paris and after he earned his law degree he began taking art lessons. He studied the style of the Old Masters, the technique of the Impressionists, and the work of sculptors. By 1900, Matisse was the leader of the Postimpressionists and was known as an Expressionist. He experimented with bright, bold colors and was interested in conveying emotions. In 1905 Matisse, along with a group of painters, had an art show. One art critic felt that the bright colors, heavy outlines, and distorted shapes that the artists used resembled the work of wild beasts. From then on, the artists were known by the French name "Fauvres," meaning wild beasts. Although Matisse did paint landscapes and flowers, it was the human form he loved most. His wife and children modeled for him often. The simplicity of form and the use of vibrant, cheerful colors characterize Matisse's paintings. His works are joyful, rhythmic, and reflect his love of color and nature. Pretty women in colorful costumes were a favorite subject matter, as well as fruits and flowers. He controlled his use of color, line, and shape so that his compositions seem to be shallow when the subjects were arranged as flat patterns.

When Matisse grew old, he was ill and confined to bed. Since it was difficult to paint, he started making paper cutouts. He used both the positive shapes and the negative spaces that were left over in his collages. These cutout compositions have bold, flat color, intriguing shapes, and incredible design techniques. Matisse died at age eighty-four.

Flower Painting

OBJECTIVES/CONCEPTS:

1. To paint in the Fauvre style, using bright, bold colors and dark outlines.
2. To focus on the flowers in Matisse's painting, *Purple Robe and Anemones,* as the subject for painting.
3. To use lines and colors for patterns.
4. To experiment with painting techniques.

MATERIALS:

12 in. x 18 in. white or manila paper
Tempera paints in a variety of colors, as well as black and white
Paintbrush

ALTERNATE MATERIALS:

Watercolor paints, crayons, oil crayons, chalk

ACTIVITIES/PROCESS:

1. View and discuss Henri Matisse's work as a Fauvre, focusing on his painting, *Purple Robe and Anemones.*
2. With the paper held vertically, mark halfway down with a pencil dot. Paint a vase from this dot to the bottom of the paper, so that it fills up half of the paper.
3. Paint one flower to fill the top part of the paper. Leaves and a stem may be added.
4. Divide the space around the flower and vase into four areas, to be filled in with four different painted patterns.
5. Outline everything with black paint, including the patterns on the vase and in the background.

QUESTIONS FOR DISCUSSION:

Why do you think Matisse used bright, bold colors in this painting? Why would he use so many patterns? Which patterns do you like? What do you notice in the picture? Do you think he chose a good title for his picture? What else could he have named it?

SHARE TIME/EVALUATION:

_____
_____
_____
_____

CURRICULUM CONNECTION:

Social Studies, Science, Language Arts

Matisse, Henri. *Purple Robe and Anemones.* (1937). Oil on canvas, 73.1 × 60.3 cm. The Baltimore Museum of Art: The Cone Collection, formed by Dr. Claribel Cone and Miss Etta Cone of Baltimore, Maryland. BMA 1950.261.

Henri Matisse

Henri Matisse (1869–1954) was a French painter.

In his later years, he used scissors to create his

art forms, working with both positive and

negative shapes. Matisse felt color had an effect

on one's mood and therefore used it as a means

of expression, rather than description. He often

compared "the rhythm of cutting paper to the

spirit of jazz music." Matisse belonged to a group

that was called the "Fauvres" (wild beasts), due

to the primitive savagery of their style.

Cutouts

OBJECTIVES/CONCEPTS:

1. To listen to jazz music while working; to experience the rhythm and carry it into the pictures.
2. To focus on color relationships, design elements, repetition, and abstraction.
3. To use both positive and negative shapes and spaces.
4. To experiment with the idea of "drawing with scissors."

MATERIALS:

12 in. x 18 in. black paper
9 in. x 12 in. colored paper
Scraps of colored paper
Scissors
Glue

ALTERNATE MATERIALS:

Paper varieties, fancy-edged scissors

ACTIVITIES/PROCESS:

1. View and discuss Henri Matisse's work, focusing on his cutouts from latter years.
2. Play jazz music while the children work.
3. Glue the colored paper on top of the black paper.
4. Cut some positive and negative shapes out of colored paper scraps.
5. Arrange shapes by layering and overlapping. Some of the cutouts will go beyond and overlap the 9 x 12 paper.
6. Glue down.

QUESTIONS FOR DISCUSSION:

What do you notice about some of the shapes in Matisse's work? What do you notice about their edges? Can you find some shapes with spaces cut out in the middle? Matisse is known for "drawing with scissors." What does that mean? Are there any shapes that are on top of each other?

SHARE TIME/EVALUATION:

_____
_____
_____
_____

CURRICULUM CONNECTION:

Music, Math

Cutouts with Printed Border

OBJECTIVES/CONCEPTS:

1. To listen to jazz music while working; to experience the rhythm and carry it into the pictures.
2. To focus on color relationships, design elements, repetition, and abstraction.
3. To use both positive and negative shapes and spaces.
4. To experiment with the idea of "drawing with scissors."
5. To print a patterned border around the collage.

MATERIALS:

9 in. x 24 in. white drawing paper

Seven pieces of 3 in. x 4 in. colored paper,
   in different colors

Scraps of colored paper

Scissors

Glue

Premade stamps, either rubber, sponge, or potato cuts

Ink pads

ALTERNATE MATERIALS:

Paper varieties, tempera paint

ACTIVITIES/PROCESS:

1. View and discuss Henri Matisse's work, especially the cutouts from the latter years.
2. Glue the seven rectangle pieces of paper to the 9 x 24 paper, so that there is a white edge all around.
3. Cut some positive and negative shapes out of colored paper scraps. Have a theme in mind that can be simplified and abstracted, such as the ocean or the sky.
4. Arrange shapes by layering and overlapping. Some of the cutouts will go beyond a rectangle's edges and overlap the next one.
5. Glue down.
6. Print the stamps around the edges to create a border.

QUESTIONS FOR DISCUSSION:

Does listening to music give us a special feeling while we work? How does it add to the free-flowing feeling of the objects? Where can you find positive shapes and where can you see some negative shapes? Is there any overlapping? Why do you think we should overlap someplace in our work? What happens when we print?

SHARE TIME/EVALUATION:

_____

_____

_____

_____

CURRICULUM CONNECTION:

Music, Math, Science, Social Studies

Matisse, Henri. *Les Codomas from Jazz.* (1947). Color stencil lithographs, 16½″ × 12¾″. Gift of Virginia and Bruce B. Dayton. 1982. The Minneapolis Institute of Arts.

Free-Flowing
Rhythm Block Design

OBJECTIVES/CONCEPTS:

1. To experience line, shape, and movement by creating free-flowing rhythm block designs.
2. To work with organic lines and shapes similar to those of Matisse.
3. To work with both positive and negative shapes.

MATERIALS:

8 in. x 10 in. white drawing paper
One colored marker per student

ALTERNATE MATERIALS:

Crayons, colored pencils, oil crayons

ACTIVITIES/PROCESS:

1. View and discuss Henri Matisse's work, especially his cutouts.
2. Divide the paper into sixteen blocks by folding the paper in half one way and then in half again. Then fold the other way in half and in half again. For preschool children, lines can be already drawn on the paper.
3. In the first block, draw a free-flowing line from one corner diagonally across to the other bottom corner. Draw a diagonal, organic-type line in each of the other blocks. Vary the direction of the line by sometimes drawing from the top left to the bottom right and sometimes from the top right to the bottom left.
4. Once all the lines have been drawn, go back and color in half of each block. Vary the halves that are colored in, by sometimes choosing the top right section and sometimes the bottom right or the top left or bottom left. Remember to use only one color of marker.

QUESTIONS FOR DISCUSSION:

What gives the feeling of movement and rhythm? Would it be the same feeling if the lines were not free-flowing lines? What about if the lines went across instead of diagonally? What does organic mean? What would happen if we used more than one color?

SHARE TIME/EVALUATION:

_____
_____
_____
_____

CURRICULUM CONNECTION:

Science, Music, Math

Joan Miró

Joan Miró was born in 1893 in Spain, to a family of craftsmen. He attended art school for three years and then left to become an apprentice to an accountant. His family had convinced him to leave school because they didn't think he was going to make it as an artist. Miró became ill; when he was well again he went back to art school and was encouraged by his teachers. Miró moved to Paris in the 1920s and became associated with the Surrealists. He developed his own personal style based on dreams, memories, and fantasies. Miró is known as the originator of an organic and abstract style of Surrealism. No matter how bizarre, the content of his pictures points back to the real world. Miró's works portray wit, exaggeration, abstraction, and whimsy. They are simple, with an emphasis on line, color, shape, symbols, and space. Miró's symbols often look like they could have been done by a child, but they have control and sophistication. The arrangement of shapes and colors suggests a system of chance; however, each symbol is not only interesting by itself, but also has a relationship with others.

Drawing

OBJECTIVES/CONCEPTS:

1. To create a drawing in the childlike, Surrealist style of Miró.
2. To use overlapping lines, primary colors, and dreamlike figures.
3. To select a title for the work.

MATERIALS:

12 in. x 18 in. white drawing paper
Markers (red, yellow, blue, and black)

ALTERNATE MATERIALS:

Crayons, oil crayons

ACTIVITIES/PROCESS:

1. View and discuss Joan Miró's work.
2. Choose a theme or title like one of Miró's, and with black marker draw lines, shapes, and figures to represent it. Add on some little figures, animal shapes, and scribbles.
3. Color in with primary-color and black markers.

QUESTIONS FOR DISCUSSION:

What kind of lines can you see? Name some of the shapes. What happens when a line crosses itself or another line? Can you find some shapes that were made this way?

SHARE TIME/EVALUATION:

_____
_____
_____
_____

CURRICULUM CONNECTION:

Math, Language Arts

Miro, Joan (1893–1983). *Woman and Bird in the Moonlight.* (1949). Tate Gallery, London, Great Britain. © 1998 Artists Rights Society (ARS), New York/ADAGP, Paris.

Joan Miró

Joan Miró (1893–1983), a Spanish artist, painted in the Cubist style for a time, and then became a member of the Surrealist group. His flat two-dimensional paintings had the sort of Surrealist distortions in which part of one person might become a part of another person. He used primary colors with a primitive, childlike line quality. He used fish, bird, and animal forms, along with aimless scribbles and strange, dreamlike figures. Miró was interested in dreams and the subconscious, and his work evokes the power of the imagination.

Amedeo Modigliani

Amedeo Modigliani was born in a ghetto in Italy in 1884. His baker father died young. His mother took him to many museums and he quickly learned to draw and paint. In 1906, Modigliani went to Paris. He lived an enjoyable life, but he had tuberculosis and his poor health shortened his life. He was inspired by the simple figures used to represent animals and people in African art and used a similar technique in his paintings. Elongated, angular lines with almost a sculptured feeling are part of his own style. Although he was influenced by African sculpture, Cubism, and Paul Cézanne's artwork, he was not part of any particular art movement. When Modigliani was out of funds, he lived and painted in the studios of his artist friends. Modigliani died at age thirty-six.

Portrait of a Woman

OBJECTIVES/CONCEPTS:

1. To create a painting in the style of Amedeo Modigliani.
2. To paint a portrait of a woman with an elongated oval head, thin nose and neck, oval-shaped eyes, and sloping shoulders.
3. To experiment with painting techniques.

MATERIALS:

12 in. x 18 in. white drawing paper
Tempera paints in primary colors (red, yellow, and blue) and black and white
Paintbrush

ALTERNATE MATERIALS:

Watercolor paints, oil crayons, chalk

ACTIVITIES/PROCESS:

1. View and discuss Amedeo Modigliani's work.
2. Paint a long oval face and long thin neck with olive or golden paint.
3. Use sloping shoulders when making the upper body. Paint the clothing.
4. Add the facial features of a long, thin nose and oval-shaped eyes.
5. Paint the background a solid color, representing a wall.

QUESTIONS FOR DISCUSSION:

What shape is the face in Modigliani's work? Can we guess how the person is feeling? What can we do in our pictures to show how people are feeling? Did you mix any colors together to get other colors? What were they and what did they make?

SHARE TIME/EVALUATION:

_____
_____
_____
_____

CURRICULUM CONNECTION:

Science, Social Studies

Modigliani, Amadeo. *Anna Zborowska.* (1917). Oil on canvas, 51¼ × 32″ (130.2 × 81.3 cm). The Museum of Modern Art, New York. Lillie P. Bliss Collection. Photograph © 1999 The Museum of Modern Art, New York.

Amedeo Modigliani

Amedeo Modigliani (1884–1920) was born

in Italy and painted portraits in a stylized

manner. The people in his paintings have

elongated oval faces, long slender necks,

sloping shoulders, golden or olive-toned

Italian skin, and a somewhat dreamy look.

He sometimes portrayed his subjects with

empty eyes and a vague expression.

Piet Mondrian

Piet Mondrian was born in Holland in 1872. His early work depicted realistic landscapes. He went through a symbolist phase before moving to Paris in 1911, where he started using Cubist ideas in an abstract way. In 1914 he moved back to Holland, and with Theo van Doesburg cofounded the De Stijl movement. The artists' work in this group emphasized the dominance of humans over the random forms of nature. Clarity and order were paramount, and accomplished by using straight lines, right angles, and the primary colors of red, yellow, and blue. In 1919, Mondrian moved back to Paris and developed his own abstract style. He created pictures based on the simplest elements of horizontal and vertical lines; with primary colors and black and white he reflected his vision of the order of the universe.

Painting

OBJECTIVES/CONCEPTS:

1. To create in the De Stijl style, using only horizontal and vertical lines in the primary colors and black.
2. To experiment with painting techniques.

MATERIALS:

12 in. x 18 in. white drawing paper
Pencils
Ruler
Tempera paint in primary colors (red, yellow, and blue) and black
Paintbrush

ALTERNATE MATERIALS:

Watercolor paints, crayons, oil crayons, markers

ACTIVITIES/PROCESS:

1. View and discuss Piet Mondrian's work.
2. Draw straight lines with a pencil and ruler, horizontally and vertically breaking up space into squares and rectangles.
3. Paint in with primary colors, leaving some spaces white.
4. Go over all lines with black paint.

QUESTIONS FOR DISCUSSION:

What are the primary colors and why are they called primary colors? Why do you think Mondrian used primary colors? Why did he use only horizontal and vertical lines? Does his work look balanced? Why or why not? What shapes are made from the lines?

SHARE TIME/EVALUATION:

_____
_____
_____
_____

CURRICULUM CONNECTION:

Math, Social Studies

Mondrian, Piet. *Composition.* (1929) Oil on canvas, 45.1 × 45.3 cms (17¾ × 17⅞ in.). Solomon R. Guggenheim Museum, New York. Gift from Estate of Katherine S. Dreier, 1953. Photograph by David Heald © The Solomon R. Guggenheim Foundation, New York.

Piet Mondrian

Piet Mondrian (1872–1944), a Dutch

painter, cofounded the De Stijl movement.

The De Stijl movement used geometric, abstract

shapes and primary colors, and was based

on the idea of universal harmony.

———————

Mondrian's *Broadway Boogie Woogie* reflected

the hurried pace of urban life in America.

Mondrian used the technique of blocking out

with tape to help keep his lines straight; in this

particular work, some of the pieces of tape are

still on the painting, leading us to believe it was

unfinished when he died in 1944. It is vibrant and

shows complication. The lines and colors seem

to move throughout the painting.

Picture

OBJECTIVES/CONCEPTS:

1. To create in the De Stijl style, using only horizontal and vertical lines in the primary colors and white and black.
2. To work with cut-paper techniques.

MATERIALS:

12 in. x 18 in. white paper
1/2-inch strips of paper in red, yellow, blue, and black
6 in. x 9 in. squares of red, yellow, blue, and black paper
Scissors
Glue

ACTIVITIES/PROCESS:

1. View and discuss Piet Mondrian's work.
2. Fill white paper with red, yellow, and blue papers, cutting them to make different-sized squares and rectangles. Leave some spaces white.
3. Place straight black strips horizontally and vertically around the colored and white shapes.
4. Small dashes of color can be added on top of the black lines.

QUESTIONS FOR DISCUSSION:

Why did Mondrian only use horizontal and vertical lines? How do you think the lines and shapes could represent a city? What makes the picture seem organized? Why do you think he only used primary colors?

SHARE TIME/EVALUATION:

_____
_____
_____
_____

CURRICULUM CONNECTION:

Math, Social Studies

Claude Monet

Claude Monet was born in Paris, France in 1840. When he was in his teens, he was paid to draw pictures of people because he was very good at it. He enjoyed drawing and continued until he met an artist named Eugene Boudin, who convinced Monet to try painting. Most artists at this time painted in studios, but Boudin thought artists should paint outdoors and Monet loved that idea. Many of Monet's pictures have water as their subject because he loved the way it reflected colors.

During this time period in Paris, most artists painted battle scenes or events in history using clear, sharp lines and dark colors. Monet and his friends were more interested in the aesthetic quality of their chosen subjects; they painted everyday things like boats and oceans and even haystacks.

These artists were called Impressionists, after the title of one of Monet's paintings called *Impression: Sunrise.* The painting glows with the colors of the sun and the sky, reflected on the water and the city. Even though most people did not like the way Monet painted, he continued undeterred. He tried to make the colors and the light and the shadows very real on the everyday scenes he painted. When looking very closely at Monet's paintings, the many colorful brush strokes seem chaotic and random. Stepping back, the picture becomes clear. Monet often painted the same subject at different times of day to see how the changing lighting affected the picture.

When Monet was older, people began to finally appreciate his work. He moved to Giverny, France, and installed beautiful gardens. He spent the last ten years of his life painting pictures of his water gardens, which are now his most famous work. He was able to convey just how things looked to him at a particular moment in time. Later in life Monet developed cataracts and painted most of his work in the color red—the only color he could see. Monet died at age eighty-six. His home and gardens have since been made into a museum.

Water Lilies

OBJECTIVES/CONCEPTS:

1. To create a painting featuring water lilies in Monet's Impressionistic fashion.
2. To mix and blend colors.
3. To experiment with painting techniques.

MATERIALS:

12 in. x 18 in. light purple or light blue paper
Tempera paints in primary colors (red, yellow, and blue) and white and black

ALTERNATE MATERIALS:

Watercolor paints, oil crayons, chalk

ACTIVITIES/PROCESS:

1. View and discuss Claude Monet's work, especially his water lilies.
2. Using dashes of paint and dabs of color, mix, blend, and paint a pond with water lilies.
3. Leave some of the paper showing through to give a shimmering effect. A Japanese footbridge can be added if desired.

QUESTIONS FOR DISCUSSION:

What makes Monet's work seem to shimmer? What ways did you make new colors? What happens when dashes of different-colored paint were used next to each other?

SHARE TIME/EVALUATION:

_____
_____
_____
_____

CURRICULUM CONNECTION:

Social Studies, Science

Monet, Claude. *Nymphéas* (Water Lilies). (1920-21). Oil on canvas, 77¹⁵⁄₁₆ × 234⁷⁄₈ in. (198 × 596.6 cm). Carnegie Museum of Art, Pittsburgh. Acquired through the generosity of Mrs. Alan M. Scaife.

Claude Monet

Claude Monet (1840–1926) was a French

Impressionist painter. He installed a water garden

in his home in Giverny and painted many

variations of the lighting across the surface of the

pond. He achieved a shimmering effect by using

individual brush strokes of different colors. He

painted his water lilies and the pond in all

seasons and in all types of weather, at many

different times of the day.

Monet, Claude. *Water Lily Pond.* © National Gallery Publications Limited, London.

Gardens

OBJECTIVES/CONCEPTS:

1. To create a picture featuring flowers in Monet's Impressionistic fashion.
2. To experiment with printing techniques.
3. To mix and blend colors.

MATERIALS:

12 in. x 18 in. light blue paper
Tempera paints in primary colors (red, yellow, and blue) and black and white
Paintbrush
Strips of corrugated cardboard in varying sizes (from 1/4 in. to 3 in.), cut from a cardboard box

ALTERNATE MATERIALS:

Variety of printing materials, such as small objects, sponges, erasers, buttons, tissue paper

ACTIVITIES/PROCESS:

1. View and discuss Monet's work, especially his flower and garden pictures.
2. Discuss color mixing.
3. Brush the paint onto an edge of a piece of cardboard strip.
4. Press the edge down onto the paper and lift.
5. Repeat this printing process while making a variety of flower shapes. Add leaves and stems.
6. Overlap flowers and add printed grass.

QUESTIONS FOR DISCUSSION:

Have you ever been in a flower garden? What does it look like? What does it smell like? If you are surrounded by flowers, what might make you choose certain ones to paint, print, or draw? How does the printing technique give the feeling of the Impressionist style?

SHARE TIME/EVALUATION:

_____

_____

_____

_____

CURRICULUM CONNECTION:

Science, Social Studies

Georgia O'Keeffe

Georgia O'Keeffe was born in 1887 in Wisconsin. Growing up she was very observant and independent. She had a sensitive awareness to her surroundings. At age thirteen, she knew she wanted to be an artist and took painting lessons. She was disappointed that all the different instructors she studied under wanted her to paint their way, rather than her own way. Finally, at the University of Virginia an instructor named Alon Belmont agreed with her way of thinking. He influenced her to fill space in a beautiful way. She wanted to study under Belmont's former teacher, Arthur Dow, but she needed to earn some money first. O'Keeffe worked as an art teacher in the public schools in Texas. While there she painted landscapes featuring the plains, the ocean (the Gulf of Mexico), and sunsets. She worked on her art, trying to simplify her style. She gained new inspiration while studying with Dow.

From 1916 to 1919, her work was first abstract and then became more defined and realistic. She painted her vision of the world from many unusual perspectives. Her landscapes, flowers, and still lifes were painted in a sort of Cubist-Realist style. Her favorite subject was flowers and she painted them from many different points of view: far away, very close, or just one magnified section. The paintings were simple and powerful.

In 1929, O'Keeffe went to New Mexico for the first time and fell in love with the landscape of the Southwest. She traveled there every summer to paint the bones, feathers, and desert landscapes. When her photographer husband died in 1946, she moved to New Mexico permanently. Georgia O'Keeffe painted in a semiabstract style until her death at age ninety-nine.

Flower Painting

OBJECTIVES/CONCEPTS:

1. To make an abstract flower, using O'Keeffe's large-scale detail.
2. To work with color mixing and blending.
3. To study and observe the details of a flower.
4. To experiment with watercolor techniques.

MATERIALS:

12 in. x 12 in. watercolor paper
Watercolor paints

ALTERNATE MATERIALS:

Tempera paints, Q-tips, sponges

ACTIVITIES/PROCESS:

1. View and discuss Georgia O'Keeffe's work, especially her flower pictures.
2. Closely observe a flower and all its detail. A magnifying glass can be used.
3. Paint part of a flower, enlarging it to fill all of the paper. Have it run off the edges of the paper.
4. Mix colors for tones, values, intensities, and blends.

QUESTIONS FOR DISCUSSION:

What can you see if you look closely at a flower? Are all the petals the same? How can we blend colors? Where can you see mixed colors? How do we lighten or darken a color?

SHARE TIME/EVALUATION:

_____
_____
_____
_____

CURRICULUM CONNECTION:

Science, Math

O'Keeffe, Georgia. *Black Iris.* (1926). Oil on canvas, 36 × 29⅞ in. The Metropolitan Museum of Art, The Alfred Stieglitz Collection, 1949. All rights reserved, The Metropolitan Museum of Art.

Georgia O'Keeffe

Georgia O'Keeffe (1887–1986) was

an American painter known for her

abstracted landscapes, her use of skulls

and natural forms, and her large-scale

flower paintings.

Flower Drawing

OBJECTIVES/CONCEPTS:

1. To make an abstract flower, using O'Keeffe's large-scale detail.
2. To work with color mixing and blending.
3. To study and observe the details of a flower.
4. To experiment with chalk pastel techniques.

MATERIALS:

12 in. x 18 in. white drawing paper
Chalk pastels

ALTERNATE MATERIALS:

Crayons, oil crayons

ACTIVITIES/PROCESS:

1. View and discuss Georgia O'Keeffe's work, especially her flower pictures.
2. Closely observe a flower and all its detail. A magnifying glass can be used.
3. Draw part of a flower, enlarging it to fill all of the paper. Have it run off the edges of the paper.
4. Mix colors for tones, values, intensities, and blends.

QUESTIONS FOR DISCUSSION:

What do you notice when you look closely at a flower? Does it matter if we do not draw the whole flower?
What happens when more than one color is used together?

SHARE TIME/EVALUATION:

_____

_____

_____

_____

CURRICULUM CONNECTION:

Science

Landscape with Skull

OBJECTIVES/CONCEPTS:

1. To create a New Mexican-style desert landscape with skull, like that of Georgia O'Keeffe's.
2. To observe and draw an animal skull.
3. To experiment with watercolor techniques.

MATERIALS:

12 in. x 18 in. white drawing paper
Pencils
Watercolor paints
Skull of an animal (obtain from the science teacher)

ALTERNATE MATERIALS:

Tempera paints, chalk, oil crayons

ACTIVITIES/PROCESS:

1. View and discuss Georgia O'Keeffe's work, especially her landscapes and skulls.
2. Observe and draw a skull.
3. Put the skull in a desert landscape, similar to O'Keeffe's New Mexican scenes.
4. Paint with watercolors.

QUESTIONS FOR DISCUSSION:

What makes the landscape look like a desert? Have you ever been to a warm place like the desert? Do you get a warm feeling when you look at the artwork? Why do you think there would be skulls in the desert? How can we make our colors lighter or darker?

SHARE TIME/EVALUATION:

_____
_____
_____
_____

CURRICULUM CONNECTION:

Science, Social Studies

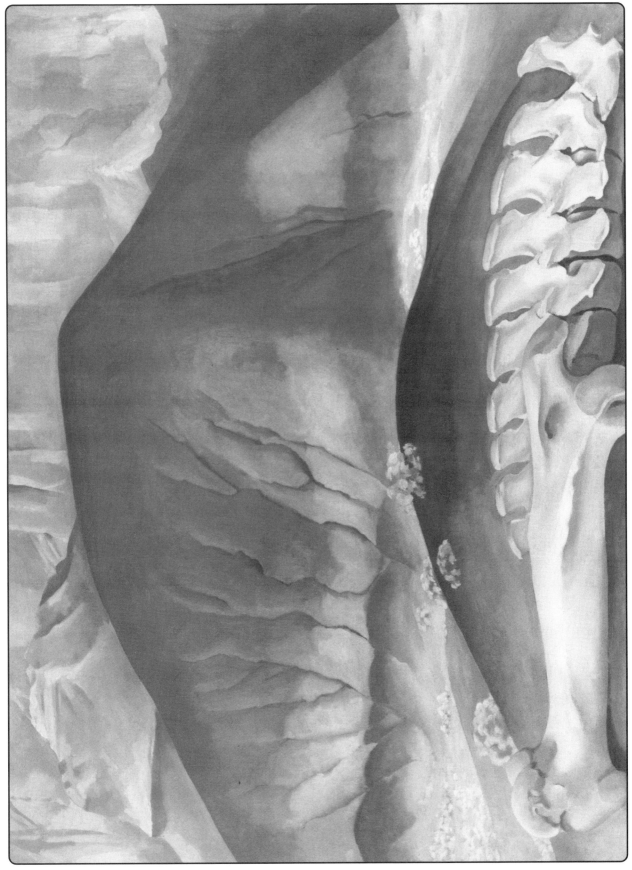

O'Keeffe, Georgia. *Red Hills and Bones.* (1941). Oil on canvas, 30" × 40". Philadelphia Museum of Art: The Alfred Stieglitz Collection. Photo by Graydon Wood, 1993.

Pablo Picasso

Pablo Picasso, one of the greatest artists of the twentieth century, was born in 1881 in Spain. His father was an art teacher and encouraged Picasso to become an artist. Over his career, Picasso's style changed more than any other artist's, for he was always trying new things. He went to Paris when he was nineteen years old and his paintings from that time resemble the work of other famous French artists, like Toulouse-Lautrec, van Gogh, Gauguin, and Monet. Then came what is called Picasso's Blue Period. His best friend died and his paintings weren't selling, so he had no money for food. He felt alone and sad. The people in his paintings looked sad and he used a lot of blue paint.

The Rose Period came next, when Picasso fell in love. He started using warm colors and happier subjects, including many paintings of animals and the circus. His next style of painting was called Cubism. The paintings look as if they have been broken up into little cubes. For many years artists had worked to make things look real, but Picasso started painting things in unrealistic ways. For example, he often painted eyes and noses in unexpected places. Cubism is an important period in the history of modern art.

Picasso painted his most serious and powerful work after a civil war in Spain. A town called Guernica and all the innocent people living there were destroyed. Picasso wanted to create a painting that would evoke the foolishness of war. Dark colors, cubism, and lots of expressive techniques were used to get his feeling across. This painting, *Guernica,* is enormous: 12 feet high and 25 feet wide. Picasso's originality made him a great artist. He died in France at the age of ninety-two.

Portrait Drawing

OBJECTIVES/CONCEPTS:

1. To create a Cubist-style portrait.
2. To become aware of facial features and proportion.
3. To work with a variety of lines, shapes, and colors to create patterned backgrounds.
4. To create textured hair using lines.

MATERIALS:

Two pieces of white drawing paper (5 1/2 in. x 17 in.)
Crayons
12 in. x 18 in. colored construction paper
Glue

ALTERNATE MATERIALS:

Oil crayons, chalk, markers

ACTIVITIES/PROCESS:

1. View and discuss Pablo Picasso's work.
2. Place two pieces of white paper side by side. Using a black marker draw a large oval, centering it so the middle of the oval is the middle edges of the paper. Add the neck and shoulders to the oval-shaped face.
3. Separate the papers and using one piece at a time, draw half a portrait on each piece. To make it more fun do not look at the other paper until both pieces are completed separately. Add all the features to each side—one eye, half a nose, an ear, half a mouth, etc. Details such as freckles, cheeks, and eyebrows can be added.
4. Create hair texture using lines: straight, curly, fluffy, wavy, etc.
5. Add lines and shapes to create patterns for clothes and background space.
6. Color in.
7. Glue the two pieces side by side onto the colored construction paper. Younger children may need assistance lining the papers up and gluing them down.

QUESTIONS FOR DISCUSSION:

By doing the two sides of the faces separately, does it seem like they are similar or different? What are some of the details that you used in your artwork? Why does it seem like there are more than one of the same kinds of facial features in Picasso's work? What kinds of patterns can you see?

SHARE TIME/EVALUATION:

_____

_____

_____

_____

CURRICULUM CONNECTION:

Science

Picasso, Pablo. *Girl Before a Mirror.* Boisgeloup, March 1932. Oil on canvas, 64 × 51¼″ (162.3 × 130.2 cm). The Museum of Modern Art, New York. Gift of Mrs. Simon Guggenheim. Photograph © 1998 The Museum of Modern Art. © 1998 Estate of Pablo Picasso/ Artists Rights Society (ARS), New York.

Pablo Picasso

Pablo Picasso (1881–1973) was born in 1881

in Spain and moved to Paris in 1901. Over his

career, Picasso's style of art changed more than

any other artist. It was Pablo Picasso, along

with Georges Braque, who invented Cubism.

Portrait Painting

OBJECTIVES/CONCEPTS:

1. To create a Cubist-style portrait.
2. To become aware of facial features and proportions.
3. To combine front view and profile view simultaneously into one portrait.
4. To work with a variety of lines and colors to create a multipatterned background.
5. To experiment with painting techniques.

MATERIALS:

12 in. x 18 in. white or manila paper
Tempera paints in primary colors (red, yellow, and blue) and black and white
Paintbrush

ALTERNATE MATERIALS:

Oil crayons, crayons, markers

ACTIVITIES/PROCESS:

1. View and discuss Pablo Picasso's work, especially his portraits.
2. Paint a portrait showing the front view and side view simultaneously.
3. Fill the background space with repeated lines and colors to make patterns. Make each side different.

QUESTIONS FOR DISCUSSION:

Why does it look as if we see the side view and the front view at the same time in Picasso's work? Is it important to put the facial features where they belong? Why do you think Picasso used patterns in his work? What kind of a feeling do you get when looking at this artwork?

SHARE TIME/EVALUATION:

_____

_____

_____

_____

CURRICULUM CONNECTION:

Science

Cut-Paper Portrait

OBJECTIVES/CONCEPTS:

1. To create a Cubist-style portrait.
2. To become aware of facial features and proportions.
3. To combine front view and profile view simultaneously into one portrait.

MATERIALS:

12 in. x 18 in. colored construction paper
9 in. x 12 in. colored construction paper
Two pieces of colored construction paper (8 in. x 11 in.)
Colored construction paper scraps
Scissors
Glue

ALTERNATE MATERIALS:

Paper varieties, material scraps, buttons, ribbon

ACTIVITIES/PROCESS:

1. View and discuss Pablo Picasso's work, especially his portraits.
2. Glue the 9 x 12 colored paper onto the center of the 12 x 18 colored paper.
3. Using the two 8 x 11 colored pieces of paper, cut both together into an oval shape.
4. Cut the edge of one of these oval shapes into a profile of a face.
5. Glue the profile view on top of the oval view, covering half the oval.
6. Using the colored paper scraps make a neck, two different eyes, one mouth, two kinds of hair and ears, etc. No other nose will be needed.
7. Glue the face down to the background paper, overlapping the 9 x 12 rectangle.

QUESTIONS FOR DISCUSSION:

How do we show a profile view? By putting the profile and the front view together, which one do you notice? Do they visually switch? Can we sense the emotions of the person being portrayed?

SHARE TIME/EVALUATION:

_____
_____
_____
_____

CURRICULUM CONNECTION:

Science

Picasso, Pablo (1881-1973). *Weeping Woman.* (1937). Oil on canvas, 23½ × 19¼ in. Tate Gallery, London, Great Britain. © 1998 Estate of Pablo Picasso/Artists Rights Society (ARS), New York.

Three-Dimensional Portrait

OBJECTIVES/CONCEPTS:

1. To create a three-dimensional, Cubist-style portrait by combining front view and profile view simultaneously.
2. To become aware of facial features and proportions.
3. To create textured hair using lines and colors.
4. To work with lines, shapes, and colors to create patterned clothes.

MATERIALS:

Two pieces of 6 in. x 9 in. oak tag (One piece should be precut into a round head, with a neck shape and a 1-inch band at the bottom for shoulders. The other piece should be cut into a profile with a 1-inch band at the bottom.)

Scissors
Black markers
Crayons

ALTERNATE MATERIALS:

Oil crayons, colored markers, glue-on eyes, buttons

ACTIVITIES/PROCESS:

1. View and discuss Pablo Picasso's work, especially his portraits.
2. On one piece of the head-shaped oak tag, draw with a black marker the front view of a portrait. Use lines, shapes, and details to add facial features and hair. Add patterned clothing on the bottom band.
3. Draw a different face on the back side of the oak tag.
4. Color a profile view on the second piece of oak tag. Decorate both sides of this piece with facial features and hair. Add patterned clothing on the bottom band.
5. Measure and cut a slit in one piece of the oak tag head, from the top down 3 inches. Measure and cut a slit in the other piece of the oak tag from the bottom up 3 inches.
6. Slide the pieces together at the slits so they will stand up when assembled.

QUESTIONS FOR DISCUSSION:

Why do we have to decorate on all the sides? What happens when we put the two pieces of oak tag together? Do the faces line up? Do they need to? What do you see when you look at it? What does it mean to be three-dimensional?

SHARE TIME/EVALUATION:

_____
_____
_____
_____

CURRICULUM CONNECTION:

Science

Jackson Pollack

Jackson Pollack was born in Wyoming in 1912. He studied art in California and in New York. Pollack changed his style of painting many times. He worked on small landscapes, but under the influence of Picasso and Miró he became more abstract. He was also influenced by the dreamlike and unrealistic style of Surrealism. He stopped doing realistic work in 1945 and focused on his subconscious mind and rhythmic movements of his body. Pollack enjoyed working on large canvases because they required the movement of his entire body. He experimented with and became the leader in a technique called "action painting," a method of pouring and splattering paint rather than applying paint with a brush. This gave the large areas of canvas complex linear patterns. Pollack's abstract paintings express feelings through unique mixtures of lines, shapes, and colors. Pollack, along with Vincent van Gogh, felt that once photography was invented there was no need to paint realistically. Although Pollack's work has a wildness to it, it was always under his control. He is considered an Abstract Expressionist. Jackson Pollack died in a car crash in 1956.

Action Painting

OBJECTIVES/CONCEPTS:

1. To create an action painting in Jackson Pollack's style.
2. To use a swirling and sweeping motion.
3. To use a variety of color.

MATERIALS:

Flat box (like the kind that holds a case of soda)
White paper that will fit into the box, approximately 10 in. x 15 in.
Tempera paints in primary colors (red, yellow, and blue) and black
Marbles
Plastic spoon
Small container for paint

ALTERNATE MATERIALS:

Paintbrush varieties, large white mural paper placed on the floor

ACTIVITIES/PROCESS:

1. View and discuss Jackson Pollack's work.
2. Put the paper in the box.
3. Put the marble in one color of paint, using the spoon to remove. Only a little paint at a time is necessary.
4. Put the marble in the box on top of the paper.
5. While standing (music can be playing in the room) use controlled sweeping and swirling motions to allow the marble to roll.
6. Dip the marble in paint whenever it gets dry.
7. If using the alternate materials, the box can be put on the floor and with the variety of paintbrushes, paint can be dribbled and spattered on the paper.

QUESTIONS FOR DISCUSSION:

Did the music make you move a certain way? What happened to the marble when the box was slightly tilted? What happened when there was a lot of paint on the marble? What happened when the marble went over a different color line?

SHARE TIME/EVALUATION:

_____
_____
_____
_____

CURRICULUM CONNECTION:

Music, Movement, Science

Pollack, Jackson. *Free Form.* (1946). Oil on canvas, 19¼ × 14″ (48.9 × 35.5 cm). The Museum of Modern Art, New York. The Sidney and Harriet Janis Collection. Photograph © 1998 The Museum of Modern Art, New York.

Jackson Pollack

Jackson Pollack (1912–1956) was an American painter whose early work was "expressionistically realistic," and then surrealistic, before becoming completely abstract and expressionistic. Pollack's "action" or "drip" paintings were created by placing the canvas on the floor and allowing the paint to fall or drip in a somewhat "controlled accident." Through sweeping gestures, the artist becomes part of the action. The pattern of lines and drips seem to change as one views the painting.

Rembrandt van Rijn

Rembrandt van Rijn was born in 1606 in Holland. Rembrandt did more self-portraits than any other artist. He used his family as many of the models for his paintings. There were no cameras in Rembrandt's time, so there was a demand for portraits. When Rembrandt was only in his twenties, he was the leading portrait painter for rich families in Amsterdam. His paintings of people seemed alive. He is well known for contrasting light and dark paints—the dark parts of his paintings make the light parts stand out. Most people in his portraits wore black clothes and serious expressions, which was the style then. But sometimes Rembrandt would dress up in bright clothes and paint himself. Rembrandt bought expensive jewelry for his wife and many props for his paintings, such as musical instruments, weapons, and so forth. He drew himself in furs and gold charms, but wore old clothes in real life. Although he is best known for his paintings of people, he also painted beautiful landscapes. Rembrandt's work eventually fell out of fashion. Being careless with his money, he went bankrupt and lived the last thirteen years of his life in poverty. Rembrandt died at the age of sixty-three.

Self-Portraits

OBJECTIVES/CONCEPTS:

1. To create a self-portrait in a realistic style.
2. To use lights and darks to portray natural lighting.
3. To portray themselves in lavish dark clothing and jewels, like the subjects in Rembrandt's portraits.
4. To work with facial features and their proportions.

MATERIALS:

12 in. x 18 in. white drawing paper
Oil crayons

ALTERNATE MATERIALS:

Crayons, tempera paints, chalk, construction paper, scissors, glue

ACTIVITIES/PROCESS:

1. View and discuss Rembrandt van Rijn's work, especially his self-portraits.
2. Discuss facial features and their proportions.
3. Draw a self-portrait as close to reality as able. Use lights, darks, and shading.
4. Dress your self-portrait in the type of clothing typical of Rembrandt's portraits.

QUESTIONS FOR DISCUSSION:

Why did artists paint portraits? Who do you think modeled for the artists? Why is it necessary to use lights and darks? When we look at the people in the portraits can you guess what type of people they are?

SHARE TIME/EVALUATION:

_____
_____
_____
_____

CURRICULUM CONNECTION:

Social Studies, Science

Rembrandt van Rijn. *Self Portrait.* (1659). Canvas/oil on canvas, .845 × .650 (33½ × 28¾). Andrew W. Mellon Collection. Photograph © 1999 Board of Trustees, National Gallery of Art, Washington, D.C.

Rembrandt van Rijn

Rembrandt van Rijn (1606–1669) was a Dutch

painter who was noted for his portraits. He was

interested in character, which he portrayed in his

portraits by painting only the essentials and using

a concentration of light. His work expressed

sincerity, truthfulness, and an understanding

of emotion. Rembrandt began painting himself

at an early age and continued making

self-portraits until the year he died.

Pierre Auguste Renoir

Pierre Auguste Renoir was born in 1841 and as a young boy showed talent for art. When he was thirteen years old he decorated plates with bouquets of flowers for a porcelain manufacturer. He enrolled in art classes and became friendly with Alfred Sisley, Claude Monet, and Frederic Bazille. They all searched for an art that was free from past traditions and closer to life. They attempted new freedoms and experimented with their style. During this time period the tradition was to paint in a studio even if the subject was a landscape. Renoir and his friends decided to go into the forest and paint directly from nature. They explored the effects of changing light on a subject. Renoir was able to suggest the vibration of atmosphere by using small multicolored brush strokes. Many of these Impressionists were frequently rejected, but Renoir, because of his interest in the human figure, was commissioned for portraits by the upper-middle-class society. Renoir painted a lot of canvases of women, children, landscapes, and flowers. He also enjoyed painting scenes from dance halls. Renoir died in 1919.

Girl with a Watering Can

OBJECTIVES/CONCEPTS:

1. To experiment with watercolor techniques.
2. To create texture with a dry brush.
3. To mix and blend colors.
4. To paint a girl in a garden holding a watering can.

MATERIALS:

9 in. x 12 in. watercolor paper
Watercolor paints
Pencils

ALTERNATE MATERIALS:

Tempera paints, colored pencils, crayons, oil crayons

ACTIVITIES/PROCESS:

1. View and discuss Pierre Auguste Renoir's work, focusing on *A Girl with a Watering Can.*
2. Draw with pencil a girl holding a watering can.
3. Using washes and the dry brush technique, paint in the grass, gardens, and pathway.
4. Paint in the girl and watering can.

QUESTIONS FOR DISCUSSION:

Why do you think artists wanted to paint outdoors? Did the artist feel it was important to paint every flower in detail? What did he do to show that there were lots of flowers? Can we tell what kind of day it was? How does the artist portray the girl? What is the difference if a dry brush is used or a brush with water on it?

SHARE TIME/EVALUATION:

_____
_____
_____
_____

CURRICULUM CONNECTION:

Science, Social Studies, Language Arts

Renoir, Pierre Auguste. *A Girl with a Watering Can.* (1876). Oil on canvas, 1.003 × .732 (39½ × 28¾). Chester Dale Collection. Photograph © 1999 Board of Trustees, National Gallery of Art, Washington, D.C.

Pierre Auguste Renoir

Pierre Auguste Renoir (1841–1919) believed that

a picture should "be a pretty thing." His paintings

show women's beauty and gentleness. Renoir

was an Impressionist who painted women and

children inside and outside in natural poses.

Renoir's landscapes and flower paintings were as

beautiful as his portraits. He always painted

flowers when they were in full bloom.

Renoir, Pierre Auguste. French, 1841-1919. *Chrysanthemums.* (1881/82). Oil on canvas, 54.7 × 65.9 cm. Mr. and Mrs. Martin A. Ryerson Collection, 1933.1173. Photograph © 1998, The Art Institute of Chicago.

Flowers in Full Bloom

OBJECTIVES/CONCEPTS:

1. To paint a vase of flowers in full bloom.
2. To experiment with painting and printing techniques.
3. To work with color mixing and blending.

MATERIALS:

12 in. x 18 in. colored paper
2 in. x 2 in. white paper, several sheets
Tempera paints in primary colors (red, yellow, and blue),
   secondary colors (green, orange, and purple), and white
Paintbrush

ALTERNATE MATERIALS:

Paper varieties, oil crayons, watercolor paints

ACTIVITIES/PROCESS:

1. View and discuss Pierre Auguste Renoir's work, especially his flower paintings.
2. Paint a large vase. A vase cutout of a kind of paper would be another option.
3. Using 2 x 2 paper, fold the paper in half and then open it back up. Dab some paint on one half, near to the fold, using more than one color. Fold in half again in order to transfer the paint to the other side. Open the paper and press onto the 12 x 18 paper to make a flower.
4. Do this several times using a different 2 x 2 paper each time.
5. Overlap the vase with a flower or two.
6. Paint the stems and leaves or use construction paper or crayons.

QUESTIONS FOR DISCUSSION:

What different shapes could the vase be? Why can the piece of paper only print once? What happens when we fold the painted paper? Is it all right if the print comes out light sometimes and dark sometimes? What gives the work a shimmering effect? What is the difference between the parts that were painted and the parts that were printed?

SHARE TIME/EVALUATION:

_____
_____
_____
_____

CURRICULUM CONNECTION:

Science

Georges Rouault

Georges Rouault was born in France in 1871. His grandfather encouraged him from childhood to become an artist. In his youth he worked with stained glass as an apprentice. This might have contributed to his strong, structural work with black contours and luminous colors. Rouault was influenced by Vincent van Gogh, Paul Gauguin, and Paul Cézanne. His work first categorized as a Fauvre due to his arbitrary use of strong color. Watercolor was his most effective medium until the beginning of World War I. After 1914, Rouault used the oil medium with thick, rich paint layers and heavy black lines resembling stained-glass windows. He mostly painted religious subjects, but he also painted a series with the theme of sorrow and sympathy. During and after World War II he painted a collection of clowns which tended to be self-portraits. Although Expressionism was not favored in France, Rouault did practice the style, but not as fiercely as his German contemporaries. He added greens and yellows to his pallet during the last ten years of his life and created mystical landscapes. Rouault died at age eighty-seven.

Sorrowful Clown

OBJECTIVES/CONCEPTS:

1. To create a clown picture with heavy black outlines, like that of a stained-glass window.
2. To try to express a sad or sorrowful feeling.
3. To experiment with painting techniques.

MATERIALS:

12 in. x 18 in. white drawing paper
Tempera paints in primary colors (red, yellow, and blue) and black and white
Paintbrush

ALTERNATE MATERIALS:

Oil crayons, chalk, markers

ACTIVITIES/PROCESS:

1. View and discuss Georges Rouault's work.
2. Paint a clown with a sad expression.
3. Use black paint to make heavy outlines around the shapes.

QUESTIONS FOR DISCUSSION:

Have you seen a stained-glass window? What makes our artwork look like the stained-glass technique? How can we make the clown look sad? What happened when you added black to a color?

SHARE TIME/EVALUATION:

_____
_____
_____
_____

CURRICULUM CONNECTION:

Social Studies, Science, Drama

Rouault, Georges. France, 1871–1958. *Profile of a Clown*. Oil on paperboard mounted on panel, 66 × 48 cm (26 × 18⅞ in.). Museum of Fine Arts, Boston (51.702). Fanny P. Mason Fund in Memory of Alice Thevin.

Georges Rouault

Georges Rouault (1871–1958), born in Paris,

served as an apprentice to a restorer of medieval

stained-glass windows when he was fourteen.

Rouault used a black heavy outline in his

paintings like the lead in the stained-glass

windows. Rouault's paintings express

powerful emotional content.

Henri Rousseau

Henri Rousseau was born in 1844. He did not begin painting until he was about forty years old, and continued to work full time as a French customs officer. Rousseau never studied art formally, but copied Old Masters and was a friend to many artists. Rousseau's simple style and untrained directness qualify him as a Primitive painter. He painted a range of subjects, which included still lifes and portraits, but his most famous paintings are jungle scenes. He based these on botanical gardens in Paris and illustrations of wild animals. After retiring from his job he painted full time. To earn money during this time, he taught music and art, and sold his paintings. Rousseau created unusual imaginary places by using ordinary objects in a surprising manner. Rousseau's inconsistency with perspective is typical of an untrained, self-taught artist. A single mysterious source of light illuminates Rousseau's balanced design, and tiny brush strokes and attention to detail are part of his style. Rousseau died poor in 1910, after accidentally cutting himself and neglecting the wound.

Jungle Scene Painting

OBJECTIVES/CONCEPTS:

1. To create a jungle scene, overlapping a variety of foliage and including at least one wild animal.
2. To create density and show space.
3. To use a variety of greens and note their differences.
4. To enlarge the perspective of the jungle so it will appear huge.
5. To work with painting techniques.

MATERIALS:

12 in. x 18 in. white paper
Tempera paints in primary colors (red, yellow, and blue), secondary colors (green, orange, and purple), and white, black, and brown
Paintbrush

ALTERNATE MATERIALS:

Watercolor paints

ACTIVITIES/PROCESS:

1. View and discuss Henri Rousseau's work, especially his jungle scenes.
2. Look at tropical forest and jungle pictures, as well as pictures of wild animals.
3. Paint large scenes filling all the paper. Mix the paints directly on the paper to allow for lots of variety. Once the paper is filled in with the shapes and colors of the foliage, go back and add textures and details. Don't forget to add an animal or two.

QUESTIONS FOR DISCUSSION:

What do you think a jungle or rain forest would look like? Notice the different shades of green in the work and see if you can tell how the colors were mixed to arrive at that particular green. Why do the animals look small? How was texture and detail added?

SHARE TIME/EVALUATION:

_____
_____
_____
_____

CURRICULUM CONNECTION:

Science, Language Arts, Social Studies

Rousseau, Henri. *The Equatorial Jungle.* (1909). Oil on canvas, 1.406 × 1.295 (55¼ × 51). Chester Dale Collection. Photograph © 1999 Board of Trustees, National Gallery of Art, Washington, D.C.

Henri Rousseau

Henri Rousseau (1844–1910) painted many

pictures of an imaginary or dream-like world. His

jungle scenes were drawn from his imagination,

and based on the vegetation of Paris' botanical

gardens and illustrations of wild animals.

Rousseau was an amateur painter who was

admired for his fresh, direct vision.

Rousseau, Henri. *The Merry Jesters* (c. 1906). Oil on canvas, 57⅜ × 44⅝″ (145.7 × 113.3 cm). Philadelphia Museum of Art: Louise and Walter Arensberg Collection.

Jungle Scene Collage

OBJECTIVES/CONCEPTS:

1. To create a jungle scene, overlapping a variety of foliage and including at least one wild animal.
2. To create density and show space.
3. To use a variety of collage materials, creating texture.
4. To use a variety of greens and note their differences.

MATERIALS:

12 in. x 18 in. black paper
Collage materials, including construction paper,
    textured papers, tissue paper, fabric material,
    yarn, burlap, etc.

ALTERNATE MATERIALS:

Oil crayons, tempera paints

ACTIVITIES/PROCESS:

1. View and discuss Henri Rousseau's work, especially his jungle scenes.
2. Look at tropical forest and jungle pictures, as well as pictures of wild animals.
3. Cut out and arrange a large jungle scene. Once the paper is filled with the shapes, colors, and textures of the foliage, go back and add little details. Don't forget to add an animal or two.

QUESTIONS FOR DISCUSSION:

What makes it look like the scene is deep in the jungle? What do you notice about the varieties of the colors? How is overlapping used? How can detail be added? If you were in the rain forest or jungle, what do you think you would see? How does the medium of collage add to the feeling of being in the jungle?

SHARE TIME/EVALUATION:

_____
_____
_____
_____

CURRICULUM CONNECTION:

Science, Social Studies, Language Arts

Georges Seurat

Georges Seurat was born in Paris, France, in 1859. He took the two important characteristics of Impressionism, bright color and effects of sunlight, one step further. Seurat was formal and reserved in his manner. He read extensively and was interested in scientific theories concerning the laws of optics, the chemistry of color, and the principles of light. He chose color combinations based on the scientific effects they had on each other as they made impressions on the eye. Seurat used an innovative painting procedure in which he used tiny brush strokes of contrasting color to portray the play of light. Up close, separate dots of color are seen but as one stands back away from the painting the eye mixes the colored dots and the correct shapes and colors of the objects are apparent. His work shows the influence of mosaics. Seurat called his procedure Divisionism, but the method is known more often as Pointillism. The tiny spots of adjacent colors gave his paintings a shimmering effect. Through the use of bright little dots of color he was able to create the illusion of volume. He spent most of his energy painting seven very large monumental paintings. Seurat's career was brief; he died at the age of thirty-one from infectious angina.

Paper Pointillism

OBJECTIVES/CONCEPTS:

1. To create a picture in Seurat's Pointillism style.
2. To apply pure dots of color next to each other and allow the eye to do the mixing.
3. To use only dots, not lines, to render shapes.

MATERIALS:

9 in. x 12 in. colored paper
Colored paper scraps
Pencils
Paper punch
Glue

ALTERNATE MATERIALS:

Art tape, sticky dots, paper varieties, confetti

ACTIVITIES/PROCESS:

1. View and discuss Georges Seurat's work.
2. After choosing a subject (animal, fish, flower, tree, bird, clown, etc.), lightly sketch the outline in pencil.
3. Punch out little dots of different colors with the paper punch.
4. Glue the dots down around the outline and fill in the shape. Add whatever details are needed with the punched dots also. Use the glue sparingly.

QUESTIONS FOR DISCUSSION:

What happens when dots of different colors are placed next to each other? Do you notice anywhere in the artwork where the colors seem to blend together? What are the colors and which color does it look like? If you look at the artwork farther away do you still notice the dots?

SHARE TIME/EVALUATION:

_____
_____
_____
_____

CURRICULUM CONNECTION:

Science

Georges Seurat

Georges Seurat (1859–1891) was a French painter

most known for his style of painting called

Pointillism, in which the canvas is painted with

dots of pure color. These colors are fused together

by the eye of the viewer and convey an

atmosphere of flickering light.

Pointillism

OBJECTIVES/CONCEPTS:

1. To create a picture in Seurat's Pointillism style.
2. To apply pure dots of color next to each other and allow the eye to do the mixing.
3. To use only dots, not lines, to render shapes.

MATERIALS:

9 in. x 12 in. white drawing paper
Colored markers
Pencils

ALTERNATE MATERIALS:

Crayons, oil crayons, colored pens, colored pencils

ACTIVITIES/PROCESS:

1. View and discuss Georges Seurat's work.
2. After choosing a subject (animal, fish, flower, tree, bird, clown, etc.), lightly sketch the outline in pencil.
3. Fill in with little dots of colors starting around the outline and then filling in the shapes. Add whatever details are needed with dots also.

QUESTIONS FOR DISCUSSION:

What do you notice if the dots are placed close together or if they are placed farther apart? What colors blend together when we look at them? What happens if the dots are smaller or larger?

SHARE TIME/EVALUATION:

_____
_____
_____
_____

CURRICULUM CONNECTION:

Science

Printed Pointillism

OBJECTIVES/CONCEPTS:

1. To create a picture in Seurat's Pointillism style.
2. To apply pure dots of color next to each other and allow the eye to do the mixing.
3. To use only dots, not lines, to render shapes.

MATERIALS:

12 in. x 18 in. colored paper
Tempera paints in primary colors (red, yellow, and blue)
Q-tips or the back point of a paintbrush

ALTERNATE MATERIALS:

Erasers on pencils, ink pad

ACTIVITIES/PROCESS:

1. View and discuss Georges Seurat's work.
2. After choosing a subject (animal, fish, flower, tree, bird, clown, etc.), lightly sketch the outline in pencil.
3. Fill in with little dots of colors starting around the outline and then filling in the shapes. Add whatever details are needed with dots also.

QUESTIONS FOR DISCUSSION:

Why did Seurat work in this style? Is it hard to tell what shapes are being made with the dots? Does it make a difference if the dots are close together or farther apart? What happens if you move close to the picture or farther away from it? Can you find areas where primary colors blend into the secondary colors? What happens if there is too much paint on the tip?

SHARE TIME/EVALUATION:

_____

_____

_____

_____

CURRICULUM CONNECTION:

Science

Vincent van Gogh

Vincent van Gogh was born in 1853 in Holland. He worked many other jobs before deciding to become an artist. He was a teacher, worked in a bookstore, and was a preacher. Van Gogh's early drawings and paintings were of the poor people he had come in contact with when he was a preacher. They have strong lines and shapes and express much feeling. He chose dark colors to portray the hard times of these people. Later he was influenced by Japanese artwork and his paintings became more colorful.

Van Gogh and his younger brother, Theo, were close and wrote letters often. It is through some of these letters that we have learned more about Vincent van Gogh. Because of his sending the letters, he came to paint the famous portrait of the postman. In 1886, van Gogh moved to Paris to be near his brother. Since Theo had a job buying and selling paintings for an art gallery he introduced Vincent to a lot of painters. Later van Gogh moved from Paris to Arles to paint. He thought it would be a great place for artists to get together, paint, and discuss their work. He could only convince one artist to go with him—Paul Gauguin. They did things differently and argued a lot, so Gauguin went back to Paris. Van Gogh had bouts of mental illness, when he became depressed and unable to control his feelings. It is thought that one time after a fight with Gauguin, van Gogh cut off part of his ear.

Van Gogh was an Expressionist, and his paintings reflect strong feelings. He put his paint on very thick and sometimes did not mix his colors. Using quick brush strokes, he used pure colors with strong contrasts in order to evoke emotion. His brush strokes make his subjects appear to be moving.

Van Gogh acted differently from most people and he became an outcast. He was poor and his brother Theo supported him. At the age of thirty-seven, after being in and out of asylums, he shot himself. Theo was devastated and died six months later due to sorrow and stress.

Starry Night Painting

OBJECTIVES/CONCEPTS:

1. To examine van Gogh's painting *The Starry Night,* attempting to understand his emotions and feelings as he looked out the window of his asylum room at the stars in the sky.
2. To try to reproduce van Gogh's painting in the Expressionist style, using an emotional quality in line, shape, and color.
3. To experiment with painting techniques.

MATERIALS:

18 in. x 24 in. white drawing paper
Tempera paints in primary colors (red, yellow, and blue) and black and white
Paintbrush

ALTERNATE MATERIALS:

Soap flakes, flour, or cornstarch can be added to the paint, which will thicken it.

ACTIVITIES/PROCESS:

1. View and discuss Vincent van Gogh's work, focusing on *The Starry Night.*
2. Paint swirling lines and dashes for brush strokes.
3. Mix the paint directly on the paper.
4. Try to paint the swirls, dabs, and dashes so they resemble stars in the sky at night.

QUESTIONS FOR DISCUSSION:

What do you notice about the texture of van Gogh's artwork? How do you think he created the texture? What kind of feeling do you get when looking at his work? Can you find areas of color that blend when you look at them?

SHARE TIME/EVALUATION:

_____

_____

_____

_____

CURRICULUM CONNECTION:

Science, Social Studies, Language Arts

van Gogh, Vincent. *The Starry Night.* (1889). Oil on canvas, 29 × 36¼″ (73.7 × 92.1 cm). The Museum of Modern Art, New York. Acquired through the Lillie P. Bliss Bequest. Photograph © 1998 The Museum of Modern Art, New York.

Vincent van Gogh

Vincent van Gogh (1853–1890) was a

Dutch painter who loved nature and saw

beauty in simple things. He painted with

swirling sweeps of color and movement.

His colors are intense and his canvases

are full of emotion and expression.

Starry Night Crayon Resist

OBJECTIVES/CONCEPTS:

1. To examine van Gogh's painting *The Starry Night,* attempting to understand his emotions and feelings as he looked out the window of his asylum room at the stars in the sky.
2. To try to reproduce van Gogh's painting in the Expressionist style, using an emotional quality in line, shape, and color.
3. To use crayon lines to represent brush strokes.
4. To experiment with crayon-resist technique.

MATERIALS:

12 in. x 18 in. white drawing paper
Crayons
Blue tempera paint, watered down
Paper towels

ALTERNATE MATERIALS:

Oil crayons, permanent markers, watercolor paints

ACTIVITIES/PROCESS:

1. View and discuss Vincent van Gogh's work, focusing on *The Starry Night.*
2. Draw with crayons, using swirling lines and dashes to represent brush strokes. Do not color anything solid, but only use dashes of lines. Bear down to get a good coating of the wax crayon. Try to copy the scene just as van Gogh depicted it.
3. Paint directly over the drawing, using quick, side-to-side brush strokes, until the paper is covered.
4. Wipe dry with a paper towel.

QUESTIONS FOR DISCUSSION:

What was it like to work with dashes rather than lines? How is it similar to the texture of van Gogh's work? Why do you think that people didn't like his work at first? What happened when you painted over the crayon marks?

SHARE TIME/EVALUATION:

_____
_____
_____
_____

CURRICULUM CONNECTION:

Science, Social Studies, Language Arts

Starry Night Mosaic

OBJECTIVES/CONCEPTS:

1. To examine van Gogh's painting *The Starry Night,* attempting to understand his emotions and feelings as he looked out the window of his asylum room at the stars in the sky.
2. To try to reproduce van Gogh's painting in the Expressionist style, using an emotional quality in line, shape, and color.
3. To experiment with paper mosaics.

MATERIALS:

9 in. x 12 in. white drawing paper
1/4 in. x 1 in. rectangles of colored construction paper,
    arranged in containers by color
Glue
Pencils

ALTERNATE MATERIALS:

Paper varieties

ACTIVITIES/PROCESS:

1. View and discuss Vincent van Gogh's work, focusing on *The Starry Night.*
2. Draw lightly with pencil where the stars, the bush, the mountains, and the church will be. Try to envision the scene just as van Gogh viewed it.
3. Glue directly over the drawing, overlapping and turning the rectangles until the whole paper is covered with pieces of mosaic.

QUESTIONS FOR DISCUSSION:

Why do you think van Gogh painted with so much texture? What do you think he was thinking when he painted this picture? How does the way this mosaic project look compare to how his work looks?

SHARE TIME/EVALUATION:

_____
_____
_____
_____

CURRICULUM CONNECTION:

Science, Social Studies, Language Arts

van Gogh, Vincent. Dutch, 1853-1890. *Bedroom at Arles.* (1888). Oil on canvas, 73.6 × 92.3 cm. Helen Birch Bartlett Memorial Collection, 1926.417. Photograph © 1998 The Art Institute of Chicago. All rights reserved.

Bedroom

OBJECTIVES/CONCEPTS:

1. To relate to van Gogh's painting *Bedroom at Arles,* attempting to understand his emotions and feelings as he viewed his somewhat cramped living space.
2. To experiment with collage techniques.
3. To create a picture of a bedroom, placing his or her self-portrait on the wall.

MATERIALS:

12 in. x 18 in. white drawing paper	Markers
Wallpaper	Glue
Construction paper scraps	Pencils
Crayons	Scissors

ALTERNATE MATERIALS:

Paper varieties, pieces of scrap material, burlap, magazines

ACTIVITIES/PROCESS:

1. View and discuss Vincent van Gogh's work, focusing on *Bedroom at Arles.*
2. Discuss things found in their own bedrooms.
3. Set up the room by cutting two pieces of wallpaper for two walls. One wall will go across the top third of the paper. The other wall will come down at an angle to the lower right-hand corner.
4. Add a door and window with construction paper. The floor can be colored in with crayons.
5. Add the bed and bureau, rug, etc., with construction paper.
6. On a small square of white paper, make a self-portrait with pencil and crayons. Frame it with colored paper and glue it to the wall.

QUESTIONS FOR DISCUSSION:

What does van Gogh's bedroom look like? Do you find it similar to your bedroom? Why do you think he has a self-portrait on the wall? Why do you think he painted his room? How does the collage work lend itself to this artwork?

SHARE TIME/EVALUATION:

_____

_____

_____

_____

CURRICULUM CONNECTION:

Social Studies, Language Arts

van Gogh, Vincent. *Sunflowers.* © National Gallery Publications Limited, London.

Sunflowers

OBJECTIVES/CONCEPTS:

1. To experiment with collage techniques to represent van Gogh's *Sunflowers.*
2. To demonstrate a variety of cutting and tearing techniques to create the textures of the flowers.
3. To use a variety of yellows and note the differences.
4. To create the composition by layering and overlapping.

MATERIALS:

12 in. x 18 in. light yellow paper
4 in. x 12 in. darker yellow paper
9 in. x 12 in. medium yellow paper
Construction paper scraps

Yellow, gold, orange, and tan papers
Green, black, and brown papers
Scissors
Glue

ALTERNATE MATERIALS:

Paper varieties, material, dried flowers, buttons, pipe cleaners

ACTIVITIES/PROCESS:

1. View and discuss Vincent van Gogh's work, concentrating on *Sunflowers.* Sunflowers were one of van Gogh's favorite subjects. They symbolized gratitude.
2. Glue the 4 x 12 strip to the bottom of the paper for the table.
3. Fold the 9 x 12 paper in half and cut out half a vase, only cutting on the open edge, not the folded edge. Open and glue onto the table.
4. Experiment with a variety of cutting and tearing techniques to create texture in the flowers.
5. Layer and overlap the flowers' shapes.
6. Add some stems and leaves.
7. Glue flowers and stems onto the vase.

QUESTIONS FOR DISCUSSION:

How are the colors in the artwork similar and different from each other? Tell about the colors that you used in your work. Where do you see overlapping? Point out some different ways you cut or tore the paper to make the flowers. How are the flowers arranged?

SHARE TIME/EVALUATION:

_____
_____
_____
_____

CURRICULUM CONNECTION:

Science, Language Arts, Math

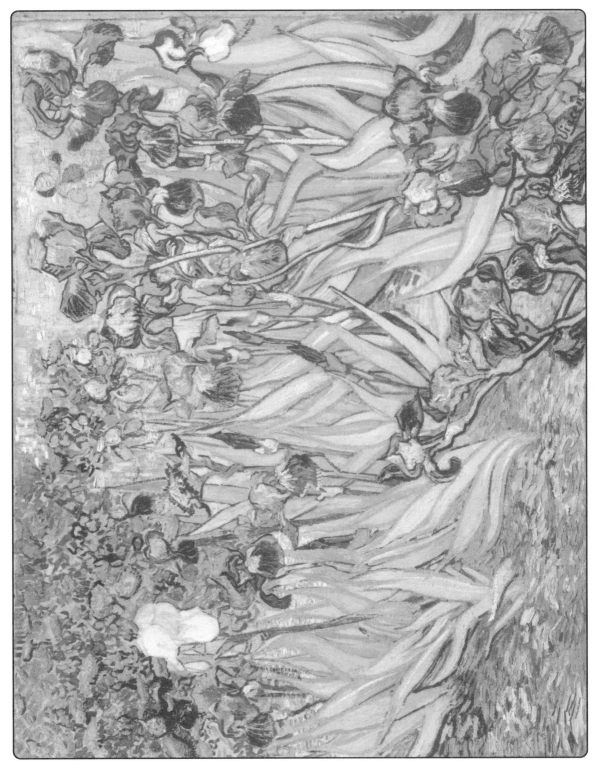

van Gogh, Vincent. *Irises.* The J. Paul Getty Museum, Los Angeles.

Irises

OBJECTIVES/CONCEPTS:

1. To examine van Gogh's painting *Irises*, attempting to understand his emotions and feelings as he painted irises in the garden of the asylum he was in.
2. To work in an Expressionist style, experimenting with printing and painting techniques.
3. To experiment with mixing colors.

MATERIALS:

12 in. x 18 in. white drawing paper
Tempera paints in primary colors (red, yellow, and blue) and secondary colors (green, orange, and purple)

ACTIVITIES/PROCESS:

1. View and discuss Vincent van Gogh's work, focusing on *Irises*.
2. Review printing techniques.
3. The object to be printed will be the side of the pinkie finger down the outside edge of the palm. Both hands will be used.
4. Paint the pinkie and edge of the palm on one hand, press and lift. This will make one side of the iris. Repeat with the other hand. Press close enough to make them look like petals on the same flower.
5. Use a fingertip to make the bottom petals that are bent backwards.
6. With a paintbrush, paint the stems, leaves, and grass.
7. Add yellow details to the inside of the irises.

QUESTIONS FOR DISCUSSION:

What does it mean to make a print? How does the shape of the edge of your hand relate to the shape of an iris? What if you had too much paint on your hand? Can you find areas of overlapping? Should all the flowers be the same height? How did you make different types of green?

SHARE TIME/EVALUATION:

_____
_____
_____
_____

CURRICULUM CONNECTION:

Science

Andy Warhol

Andrew Warhol was born in Pennsylvania in 1928. He became a fashion illustrator in New York, for magazines like *Seventeen* and *Glamour.* The magazines misspelled his name as Warhol—it was actually Warhola. He and his mother lived in a series of apartments with no hot water, and between eight and twenty cats. As an artist, Warhol felt that a bizarre image would increase his sales. His trademark look included a blonde wig, large sunglasses, a black leather jacket and high-heeled boots. Warhol never married. He worked twelve hours a day in his studio and then went to parties at night. Warhol's most famous paintings were of the thirty-two varieties of Campbell's soup. There was no deep meaning to them other than the fact that he loved soup and that his mother often made them soup when they didn't have money. He liked to paint things that are used every day but never thought about. Warhol also painted portraits of people he had never met, such as his painting of Marilyn Monroe in 1962. It was his first celebrity painting, and showed his fascination with the idea of fame. Warhol died at age fifty-eight after gallbladder surgery.

Campbell's Soup Label

OBJECTIVES/CONCEPTS:

1. To view and discuss Pop Art, especially Andy Warhol's work.
2. To become aware of commercial artists, advertising issues, and label information.
3. To draw to detail from observation.
4. To practice lettering techniques.

MATERIALS:

9 in. x 12 in. white drawing paper
Colored pencils
Pencils
Can or label from Campbell's soup

ALTERNATE MATERIALS:

Markers, colored pens, charcoal pencils, variety of labels

ACTIVITIES/PROCESS:

1. View and discuss Andy Warhol's work, especially his Campbell's soup pictures.
2. Observe a Campbell's soup label. Note the lettering and logos.
3. Draw the can and label, showing all the details as close to the correct proportions as able.
4. Color in using the colors that are on the actual label.

QUESTIONS FOR DISCUSSION:

Why do you think artists wanted to paint everyday objects? Do you ever look carefully at an everyday object to really see it? Why do you think graphic artists need to think about colors and lettering? Why do you think a label is important to the product?

SHARE TIME/EVALUATION:

_____
_____
_____
_____

CURRICULUM CONNECTION:

Science, Graphic Arts

Warhol, Andy. *Campbell's Soup Can (Cream of Chicken).* (1962). Synthetic polymer paint on canvas, 71¾ × 52 in. (182.2 × 132.1 cm). The Andy Warhol Museum, Pittsburgh. Founding Collection, Contribution The Andy Warhol Foundation for the Visual Arts, Inc. © 1998 The Andy Warhol Foundation for the Visual Arts/ARS, New York. Photography by Richard Stoner 03/21/95.

Andy Warhol

Andy Warhol (1928–1987) was born in

Pennsylvania to parents who had emigrated from

Czechoslovakia. He worked as a commercial artist

and was one of the most famous Pop artists.

These artists took images from cartoons,

advertising, food industries, and entertainment

and changed them by repeating, enlarging, or

distorting them, as a way of commenting

on the use of images in Western society.

Most of Warhol's best-known work involves

repetition by means of silk-screening.

Grant Wood

Grant Wood was born on a farm in Iowa in 1832. He was an interior decorator, a metal worker, an art student, and an art teacher. He made several trips to Europe, which changed his thinking and painting style. In 1927, Wood was commissioned for a stained-glass window and traveled to Germany seeking craftsmen. During his stay Wood was influenced by the detailed paintings of the sixteenth century German and Flemish masters. His work became sharply detailed and realistic. He became a political and social radical.

Wood's best-known work is a double portrait called *American Gothic.* This is supposedly representing a farmer and his wife, in the rural surroundings of his childhood. Actually his sister and their dentist modeled for the painting. Although he painted this depiction of Midwestern life less seriously, it has over the years become a folk symbol for an era in America's past. Wood was a major Midwestern Regionalist. The movement of Regionalism flourished during the 1930s in the United States. Grant Wood died in Iowa in 1942.

Grant Wood
Activity 1

American Farm

OBJECTIVES/CONCEPTS:

1. To create a farm like the one in Wood's painting.
2. To work with a variety of textures.
3. To work with overlapping.
4. To experiment with collage techniques.

MATERIALS:

9 in. x 12 in. light blue paper
Construction paper
Corrugated paper
Wallpaper
Magazines
Glue
Scissors
Colored pencils

ALTERNATE MATERIALS:

Colored pencils, crayons, oil crayons, paints, paper varieties

ACTIVITIES/PROCESS:

1. View and discuss Grant Wood's *American Gothic*.
2. Use a variety of papers to make a farm and cottage.
3. Look through magazines to add details.
4. Using a photocopy of the two people, cut them out and glue them down.

QUESTIONS FOR DISCUSSION:

How is our architecture today similar and different from the past? What kind of feeling do you get when looking at the artwork? What do you think the people were like? Why did the artist use his sister and a local dentist as his models? How did the different materials lend themselves to the picture? What do you think a farm was like?

SHARE TIME/EVALUATION:

_____
_____
_____
_____

CURRICULUM CONNECTION:

Social Studies, Language Arts, Science

Wood, Grant. American, 1891-1942, *American Gothic.* (1930). Oil on beaverboard, 74.3 × 62.4 cm. Friends of American Art Collection, All rights reserved by the Art Institute of Chicago and VAGA, New York, NY, 1930.934. Photograph © 1998 The Art Institute of Chicago. All rights reserved.

Grant Wood

Grant Wood (1892–1942) was a so-called Regionalist, which is an artist who finds inspiration in local surroundings and executes them in a realistic manner. Wood's style was derived from the Gothic and early Renaissance masters. He spent much of his life in Iowa and painted a small Gothic-style cottage in that town. He used his sister and the local dentist as models and tried to convey the down-to-earth dignity of small-town America.

Frank Lloyd Wright

Frank Lloyd Wright was born in Wisconsin in 1867. As a boy, the prairies near the Wisconsin River first inspired him. He studied engineering, and at age twenty worked as a draftsman for a Chicago architect. Wright then joined Louis Sullivan, the inventor of the first skyscraper. He influenced Wright greatly, as he believed that an architect was "a poet who used materials, rather than words." They both believed that the form of a building should follow its function or purpose. They felt that the inside of the building should reflect the personality of its inhabitants.

Wright began his own architectural firm and designed many buildings in Chicago. He found nature to be an inspiration for his architectural structures. Wright favored a "prairie-style" design, which was open and spacious, low to the ground, and horizontal. By using lots of glass, the landscape became part of the building. He was conscious of the three-dimensional aspects of buildings and the relationship between horizontal and vertical structures. One of Wright's most famous buildings is the Guggenheim Museum in New York, which was completed in 1960. Frank Lloyd Wright died in 1959.

Architectural Drawing

OBJECTIVES/CONCEPTS:

1. To draw a "prairie-style" building.
2. To show three dimensions on a two-dimensional surface.
3. To work with tones and values.

MATERIALS:

12 in. x 18 in. white drawing paper
Pencils
Rulers

ALTERNATE MATERIALS:

Colored pencils, charcoal pencils, crayons

ACTIVITIES/PROCESS:

1. View and discuss Frank Lloyd Wright's work.
2. Draw a building, using forms such as cubes, cylinders, cones, etc.
3. Use tones and values to shade the building, giving a three-dimensional effect.

QUESTIONS FOR DISCUSSION:

What is an architect? Why is it important to know where the building is going to be before it is designed? What is the "prairie-style" building? Why did Frank Lloyd Wright like "prairie-style" architecture? How do we make something look three-dimensional? What types of forms can you find in the buildings?

SHARE TIME/EVALUATION:

_____
_____
_____
_____

CURRICULUM CONNECTION:

Science, Social Studies, Architecture

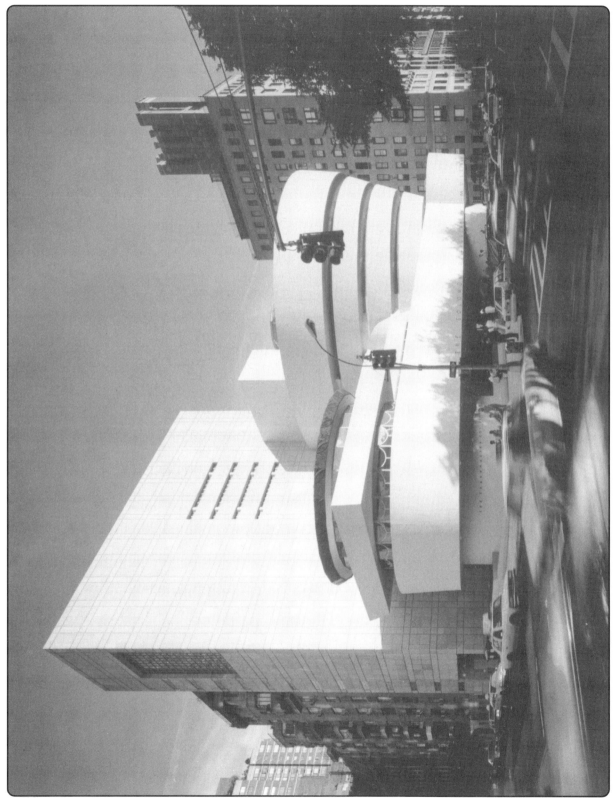

Solomon R. Guggenheim Museum, New York. (1992). Photograph by David Heald © The Solomon Guggenheim Foundation, New York.

Frank Lloyd Wright

Frank Lloyd Wright (1867–1959) was

an American architect. He thought that

architecture should resemble the forms of

nature. His "prairie-style" buildings were

open and spacious. They were low to the

ground and featured lots of glass and

porchways to incorporate the landscape.

Andrew Wyeth

Andrew Wyeth was born in Pennsylvania in 1917. His father was an illustrator and painter. During the fifties, when Abstract Expressionism was the leading style, he painted realistically and precisely. His surface texture remained delicate whether he used watercolor or tempera paints. He often used the dry brush technique. Wyeth came to Maine to paint at age twenty-two and met his future wife Betsy James. Betsy's friend Christina Olson, who was crippled from polio, lived in a farmhouse near where Wyeth painted in the summer. He looked out his window one day and saw Christina pulling herself toward the house. This was the inspiration for one of his most famous paintings. When Christina died in 1968, Wyeth no longer wanted to paint at the Olson farm. Wyeth's portraiture is realistic and expressive, exhibiting full attention to detail and texture. He painted the people of his private world over and over. Wyeth's palette is restricted to mostly earth colors, however, they have the capabilities of muted harmonies. His precise and detailed technique rises above photographic naturalism because of an unreal visionary quality. In his paintings of old houses and their interiors, Wyeth is able to communicate a sense of generations of living. Wyeth often secluded himself in his studio when he was working on a painting. Andrew Wyeth is still alive today. His youngest son Jamie is also a painter.

Girl in the Field

OBJECTIVES/CONCEPTS:

1. To create a picture similar to *Christina's World*, with a girl in a field.
2. To work with texture and detail.
3. To show distance.
4. To blend and mix colors.

MATERIALS:

9 in. x 12 in. white drawing paper
Colored pencils

ALTERNATE MATERIALS:

Crayons, chalk, watercolor paints, tempera paints

ACTIVITIES/PROCESS:

1. View and discuss Andrew Wyeth's work, focusing on *Christina's World*.
2. Draw the back view of a girl sitting in a field.
3. Put a farmhouse in the distance.
4. Add the small details of grass, using lines in a variety of greens, yellows, and browns.

QUESTIONS FOR DISCUSSION:

Have you ever looked out the window and seen something you'd like to draw? What do you think the artist was trying to show? What makes the painting realistic? How is detail used? Where can you see colors that are blended? How is distance shown?

SHARE TIME/EVALUATION:

_____
_____
_____
_____

CURRICULUM CONNECTION:

Science, Social Studies, Language Arts

Wyeth, Andrew. *Christina's World.* (1948). Tempera on gessoed panel, 32¼ × 47¾″ (81.9 × 121.3 cm). The Museum of Modern Art, New York. Purchase. Photograph © 1998 The Museum of Modern Art, New York.

Andrew Wyeth

Andrew Wyeth (1917–) has a boyish,

childlike character even in his eighties. He was

trained by his illustrator father and had his first

show at age twenty in New York. Wyeth's

portraits and landscapes are rich with emotion.

Wyeth enjoyed painting the spirit of winter.

Wyeth paints what is important to him

and never cared about being a trendsetter.

Conclusion

Children gain satisfaction and a feeling of accomplishment by expressing their ideas visually. It is an enjoyable and meaningful way for children to be spontaneous. They become more aware of themselves and their environment when they are able to express their feelings and interests visually. Through art children learn to observe, investigate, select, organize, communicate, and appreciate what they and others create. In a high-tech society, art provides a humanizing balance. Art is a way for people to share what they see, feel, and think. The artistic growth of a child, from scribbles to symbols to the desire for representation, reflects the chronological, emotional, intellectual, and perceptual growth of the child. Experimenting with materials is fascinating for children and to experiment in the style of a famous artist encourages a feeling of inventiveness, adventure, and discovery. The ideas and lessons in this book, along with the biographical information, will expand creativity in a way that all teachers can appreciate, even without a background in art.

It is important for art teachers to emphasize to their students the importance of originality. A teacher's praise for a student's expression of originality can encourage latent talents, as well as foster positive attitudes toward the whole process of learning.

Children benefit from experiencing art at an early age and from learning that art is a vital form of communication that has been part of life since the beginning of humankind. Art history can be taught by sharing pictures of artists' work along with simple information and encouraging both verbal and visual responses from children. It is important to expose children to a wide variety of artists and their work to allow for many different styles and creative expressions. After being exposed to the work of famous artists, children take pride in recognizing the artists' names and the styles with which they have become familiar.

The Great Art Detective Project

GOAL:

The project will provide a way for students to become involved with art and appreciate it as a visual form of communication.

OBJECTIVES:

- The project will expose students to the visual arts.
- The project will allow students to become informed about art.
- The project will allow students to respond to a variety of masterpieces.
- The project will stimulate critical thinking about art.
- The project will enrich oral and written expression.

SETUP:

One reproduction will be hung in every classroom for a month. A short biography of the artist will accompany it. Thought-provoking questions will be hung next to the artwork, focusing on who, what, where, when, why, and how. There will also be a look-and-find assignment. At the end of each month, the reproductions will rotate.

REWARD:

At the end of the month, classroom teachers may award students with a certificate stating they are art detectives. The student's name, along with the name of the particular reproduction and the artist, will be written down with the month that the students viewed the artwork. Other rewards can also be given, such as computer-generated certificates, ribbons, postcard reproductions, art buttons or pins, etc.

Become an Art Detective

WHO is the artist?

WHAT is the artist showing us?
WHAT materials were used?
WHAT does it make you think of or feel like?

WHEN did the artist live?
WHEN the artist created this picture what was happening in the world?

WHERE does the picture take place?

WHY did the artist choose to make this artwork?

HOW is the art similar or different from other art?
HOW does the art create interest in the viewer?
HOW do you think the artist was feeling when he or she created this work?

LOOK closely and FIND different kinds of lines, shapes, colors, and textures.

Art Detective

_____

has become an art detective for the month of _____ for successfully

observing and discussing the artwork _____

by the artist _____

Art Detective

_____

has become an art detective for the month of _____ for successfully

observing and discussing the artwork _____

by the artist _____

Art Detective

_____

has become an art detective for the month of _____ for successfully

observing and discussing the artwork _____

by the artist _____

Art Detective

_____

has become an art detective for the month of _____ for successfully

observing and discussing the artwork _____

by the artist _____

Art Materials

The following materials are used throughout the various art lessons in this book. Additional materials may be used depending on individual creativity. The materials listed are safe for children; however, adult supervision is always recommended when young children are working. Safety precautions should be utilized when children are cutting, stapling, or using sharp objects.

Aluminum foil

Beads
Brayer
Buttons

Cardboard
Cellophane
Chalk
Charcoal
Charcoal pencils
Clay
Colored pencils
Confetti
Cotton swabs
Crayons

Fabric scraps
Feathers
Foam board

Glitter
Glue

Hole punch

Ink pads

Magazines
Marbles
Markers
 washable
 permanent

fine-point
 round
Masking tape
Music

Nature items
Newspaper

Oak tag

Paint
 acrylic
 tempera
 watercolor
Paintbrushes
Paper
 bogus
 brown wrapping
 construction
 corrugated
 crepe
 metallic
 shiny
 textured
 tissue
 wallpaper
 watercolor
 white drawing
 wrapping
Paper clips
Paper towels
Pastels (chalk)

Pens
 ballpoint
 scratch
Pencils
Pointed wooden drawing tools
Printing plate

Ribbon
Ruler

Salt
Sand
Sandpaper
Scissors
 straight-edged
 fancy-edged
Scratch board
Scratch paper
Sponges
Stapler
Sticky dots
Straws
String
Styrofoam packing

Toothbrushes
Toothpicks

Wire
Wood blocks

Yarn

Art Styles

The art styles, listed below in alphabetical order, are described in more detail in Art History in Brief, a section at the front of the book. The artists contained in this book are listed under the style to which they contributed.

Abstract. A style of the 1900s that discards identifiable subject matter and is sometimes called nonobjective art or nonfigurative art.

Alexander Calder   Wassily Kandinsky   Piet Mondrian
M. C. Escher   Joan Miró

Architecture. The science or art of building. It encompasses the design, style, and qualities that distinguish buildings from one time, region, or group from those of others.

Frank Lloyd Wright

Baroque. A style of art characterized by the use of curved forms and lavish ornamentation. Baroque architecture prevailed in Europe from about 1550 to the late 1700s.

Rembrandt van Rijn

Cubism. A style of art, developed in the early 1900s, in which objects are represented by cubes and other geometrical forms instead of realistic details.

Romare Bearden   Georges Braque   Pablo Picasso

Contemporary. Marked by characteristics of the present period.

Stuart Davis

Expressionism. A style in which the art represents the artists' own reactions, regardless of tradition. Expressionists often distorted reality.

Wassily Kandinsky   Paul Klee   Jackson Pollack

Fauvism. A style that represented a radical form of expression, using brilliant colors and bold designs.

Henri Matisse   Georges Rouault

Impressionism. A style of art that conveys the impression made by the subject on the artist, without much attention paid to detail. It was developed by French painters in the late 1800s.

Mary Cassatt   Claude Monet
Edgar Degas   Pierre Auguste Renoir

Naturalism. A style of art in which there is a close adherence to nature and reality.

Albrecht Dürer

Postimpressionism. A style of art developed by a group of French artists at the end of the 1800s, which departed from Impressionism in its freer use of color, form, design, and expression.

Paul Cézanne   Henri Matisse   Georges Seurat
Paul Gauguin   Pierre Auguste Renoir   Vincent van Gogh

Pop Art. An art form that uses everyday objects, especially mass-produced objects, as its subject matter and sometimes also as the artistic medium itself.

Jasper Johns (forerunner)   Andy Warhol

Primitive. A style of art that is very simple and often untrained.

Henri Rousseau

Realism. A style of art that is based on what is real and practical. The representation of things as they exist in real life.

Winslow Homer   Georgia O'Keeffe
Edward Hopper   Andrew Wyeth

Regionalism. A style that shows a strong attachment to a certain region, or stresses regional customs or peculiarities.

Grant Wood

Renaissance. A transitional movement in Europe beginning in the fourteenth century and lasting into the seventeenth century. It was marked by a humanistic revival of classical influence expressed in a flowering of the arts and the beginnings of modern science.

Leonardo da Vinci   Albrecht Dürer

Surrealism. A movement in art that tries to show what takes place in dreams and in the subconscious mind. It is characterized by unexpected arrangements and distortions of images.

Romare Bearden   Salvador Dalí   Joan Miró
Marc Chagall   Paul Klee

Reproduction Listing

Bearden, Romare:
1. *Serenade.* Madison Art Center, Madison, Wisconsin.

Braque, Georges:
1. *Man with a Guitar.* Museum of Modern Art, New York.
2. *La table du musicien. (The Musician's Table).* Kunstmuseum, Basel, Switzerland.

Calder, Alexander:
1. *Lobster Trap and Fish Tail.* Museum of Modern Art, New York.
2. *Slanting Red Nose.* Museum of Modern Art, New York.

Cassatt, Mary:
1. *Mother Playing with Child.* Metropolitan Museum of Art, New York.

Cézanne, Paul:
1. *Still Life with Apples and Peaches.* National Gallery of Art, Washington, D.C.
2. *Still Life: Flask, Glass, and Jug.* Guggenheim Museum, New York.

Chagall, Marc:
1. *I and the Village.* Museum of Modern Art, New York.

Dalí, Salvador:
1. *The Persistence of Memory.* Museum of Modern Art, New York.

da Vinci, Leonardo:
1. *Mona Lisa.* Louvre, Paris.

Davis, Stuart:
1. *Semé.* Metropolitan Museum of Art, New York.
2. *Landscape with Garage Lights.* Memorial Art Gallery of the University of Rochester, Rochester, New York.

Degas, Edgar:
1. *Before the Ballet.* National Gallery of Art, Washington, D.C.
2. *Dancer Putting on Her Stocking.* Minneapolis Institute of Art, Minneapolis, Minnesota.
3. *The Races.* National Gallery of Art, Washington, D. C.

Dürer, Albrecht:
1. *Large Piece of Turf.* Albertina Graphische Sammlung, Vienna.

Escher, M.C.:
1. *Mosaic I.* Cordon Art-Baarn, Holland.
2. *Sky and Water I.* Cordon Art-Baarn, Holland.

Gauguin, Paul:
1 *Ta Matete (The Market).* Kunstmuseum, Basel, Switzerland.

Homer, Winslow:
1. *Breezing Up (A Fair Wind).* National Gallery of Art, Washington, D.C.
2. *Weatherbeaten.* Portland Museum of Art. Portland, Maine.

Hopper, Edward:
1. *Nighthawks.* Art Institute of Chicago, Chicago, Illinois.

Johns, Jasper:
1. *Numbers in Color.* Albright-Knox Art Gallery, Buffalo, New York.
2. *Three Flags.* Whitney Museum of American Art, New York.

Kandinsky, Wassily:
1. *Improvisation 31 (Sea Battle).* National Gallery of Art, Washington D.C.
2. *Composition 8.* Museum of Modern Art, New York.

Klee, Paul:
1. *Twittering Machine.* Museum of Modern Art, New York.
2. *Senecio (Head of a Man).* Kunstmuseum, Basel, Switzerland.

Matisse, Henri:
1. *Purple Robe and Anemones.* Baltimore Museum of Art, Baltimore, Maryland.
2. *Les Codomas from Jazz.* Minneapolis Institute of Arts, Minneapolis, Minnesota.

Miró, Joan:
1. *Woman and Bird in the Moonlight.* Tate Gallery, London.

Modigliani, Amedeo:
1. *Anna Zborowska.* Museum of Modern Art, New York.

Mondrian, Piet:
1. *Composition.* Guggenheim Museum, New York.

Monet, Claude:
1. *Nymphéas (Water Lilies).* Museum of Art, Carnegie Institute, Pittsburgh, Pennsylvania.
2. *Water Lily Pond.* National Gallery, London.

O'Keeffe, Georgia:
1. *Black Iris.* Metropolitan Museum of Art, New York.
2. *Red Hills and Bones.* Philadelphia Museum of Art, Philadelphia, Pennsylvania.

Picasso, Pablo:
1. *Girl Before a Mirror.* Museum of Modern Art, New York.
2. *Weeping Woman.* Tate Gallery, London.

Pollack, Jackson:
1. *Free Form.* Museum of Modern Art, New York.

Rembrandt van Rijn:
1. *Self-Portrait, 1659.* National Gallery of Art, Washington, D.C.

Renoir, Pierre Auguste:
1. *A Girl with a Watering Can.* National Gallery of Art, Washington, D.C.
2. *Chrysanthemums.* Art Institute of Chicago, Chicago, Illinois.

Rouault, Georges:
1. *Profile of a Clown.* Boston Museum of Fine Arts, Boston, Massachusetts.

Rousseau, Henri:
1. *The Equatorial Jungle.* National Gallery of Art, Washington, D.C.
2. *The Merry Jesters,* Philadelphia Museum of Art, Philadelphia, Pennsylvania

Seurat, Georges:
1. *A Sunday on La Grande Jatte.* Art Institute of Chicago, Chicago, Illinois.

van Gogh, Vincent:
1. *The Starry Night.* Museum of Modern Art, New York.
2. *Bedroom at Arles.* The Art Institute of Chicago, Chicago, Illinois.
3. *Sunflowers.* The National Gallery, London.
4. *Irises, 1889.* J. Paul Getty Museum, Malibu, California.

Warhol, Andy:
1. *Campbell's Soup Can (Cream of Chicken).* Andy Warhol Museum, Pittsburgh, Pennsylvania.

Wood, Grant:
1. *American Gothic.* Art Institute of Chicago, Chicago, Illinois.

Wright, Frank Lloyd:
1. Solomon R. Guggenheim Museum, New York.

Wyeth, Andrew:
1. *Christina's World.* Museum of Modern Art, New York.

Museum Listing

Albertina Graphische Sammlung (Vienna)
Augustinerstrassel
A-1010 Wien

Large Piece of Turf by Albrecht Dürer

Albright-Knox Art Gallery
1285 Elmwood Ave.
Buffalo, NY 14222

Numbers in Color by Jasper Johns

Andy Warhol Museum
117 Sandusky St.
Pittsburgh, PA 15212-5890

Campbell's Soup Can (Cream of Chicken) by Andy
  Warhol

Art Institute of Chicago
111 S. Michigan Ave.
Chicago, IL 60603-6110

Bedroom at Arles by Vincent van Gogh
American Gothic by Grant Wood
Nighthawks by Edward Hopper
Chrysanthemums by Pierre Auguste Renoir
Sunday on La Grande Jatte by Georges Seurat

Baltimore Museum of Art
Public Relations
Art Museum Dr.
Baltimore, MD 21218-3898

Purple Robe and Anemones by Henri Matisse

Carnegie Museum of Art
4400 Forbes Ave.
Pittsburgh, PA 15213-4080

Nymphéas (Water Lilies) by Claude Monet

Cordon Art
Nieuwstraat 6
P.O.Box 101
3740 AC Baarn, Holland

Mosaic I by M. C. Escher
Sky and Water by M. C. Escher

Guggenheim Museum
575 Broadway
New York, NY 10012

Still Life: Flask, Glass, and Jug by Paul Cézanne
Composition by Piet Mondrian
Solomon R. Guggenheim Museum
  by Frank Lloyd Wright
Composition 8 by Wassily Kandinsky

J. Paul Getty Museum (Malibu, California)
P.O. Box 2112
Santa Monica, CA 90407-2212

Irises by Vincent van Gogh

Kunstmuseum (Basel, Switzerland)
Offentliche Kunstsammlung Basel
St. Alban-Graben 16
Ch-4010 Basel

Ta Matete (The Market) by Paul Gauguin
Senecio (Head of a Man) by Paul Klee
La table du musicien (The Musician's Table) by
  Georges Braque

Louvre
Musée du Louvre
75058 Paris Cedex

Mona Lisa by Leonardo da Vinci

Madison Art Center
211 State St.
Madison, WI 53703

Serenade by Romare Bearden

**Memorial Art Gallery of the University
  of Rochester**
500 University Ave.
Rochester, NY 14607

Landscape with Garage Lights by Stuart Davis

Metropolitan Museum of Art
1000 Fifth Ave.
New York, NY 10028-0198

Mother Playing with Child by Mary Cassatt
Semé by Stuart Davis
Black Iris by Georgia O'Keeffe

Minneapolis Institute of Arts
2400 Third Ave. South
Minneapolis, MN 55404

Les Codomas from Jazz by Henri Matisse
Dancer Putting on Her Stocking by Edgar Degas

Museum of Fine Arts
465 Huntington Ave.
Boston, MA 02115

Profile of a Clown by Georges Rouault

Museum of Modern Art, New York
11 W. 53rd St.
New York, NY 10019

Christina's World by Andrew Wyeth
The Starry Night by Vincent van Gogh
Man with a Guitar by Georges Braque
Lobster Trap and Fish Tail by Alexander Calder
Slanting Red Nose by Alexander Calder
I and the Village by Marc Chagall
The Persistence of Memory by Salvador Dalí
Girl Before a Mirror by Pablo Picasso
Free Form by Jackson Pollack
Twittering Machine by Paul Klee
Anna Zborowska by Amedeo Modigliani

National Gallery
National Gallery
Trafalgar Square, London
WC2

Sunflowers by Vincent van Gogh
Water Lily Pond by Claude Monet

National Gallery of Art, Washington D.C.
4th St. and Constitution Ave., N.W.
Washington, D.C. 20565

Still Life with Apples and Peaches by Paul Cézanne
A Girl with a Watering Can by Pierre Auguste Renoir
Before the Ballet by Edgar Degas
The Races by Edgar Degas
The Equatorial Jungle by Henri Rousseau
Breezing Up (A Fair Wind) by Winslow Homer
Improvisation 31 (Sea Battle) by Wassily Kandinsky
Self Portrait, 1659 by Rembrandt van Rijn

Philadelphia Museum of Art
P.O. Box 7646
Philadelphia, PA 19101

Red Hills and Bones by Georgia O'Keeffe

Portland Museum of Art
Seven Congress Square
Portland, ME 04101

Weatherbeaten by Winslow Homer

Tate Gallery
Tate Gallery
Millbank, London
SW1

Woman and Bird in the Moonlight by Joan Miró
Weeping Woman by Pablo Picasso

Whitney Museum of American Art
945 Madison Ave
New York, NY 10021

Three Flags by Jasper Johns

Glossary

abstract art—A visual interpretation with little regard to realistic representation.

aesthetic—Appreciation of the beauty in art or nature.

art appreciation—Awareness of the aesthetic values in artwork.

art medium—Materials used to create an artwork.

art museum—A building where artwork is displayed.

art reproduction—Photographic duplication of an original piece of art.

asymmetrical—Artwork that looks balanced when the parts are arranged differently on each side.

background—The part of an artwork that looks farther away or is behind other parts.

balance—The arrangement of visual elements so that the parts seem to be equally important.

basic shapes—Circle, square, triangle, rectangle.

brayer—A roller used to apply paint or ink.

cityscape—A view or picture of a city.

collage—Artwork made by assembling and gluing materials to a flat surface.

composition—The arrangement of design elements.

concept—A general idea or understanding.

construct—To create an artwork by putting materials together.

contour—The outline of a shape or form.

contrast—The apparent difference between two things.

cool colors—Colors that remind people of cool things. They often create a calm or sad feeling. Blue, green, and purple are cool colors.

crayon etching—Scratching through one layer of crayon to let another layer of crayon show through.

creative—Having the ability to make things in a new or different way.

Cubism—A style of art where shapes or forms seem to be divided or have many edges.

design—The ordered arrangement of art elements in an artwork.

design elements—The basic visual tools an artist manipulates: line, shape, form, color, value, and texture.

design principles—The way an artist uses the design elements: unity, balance, rhythm, movement, variety, repetition.

detail—Small items or parts.

drawing—Describing something by means of line.

emphasis—Special stress of one or more art design components.

Expressionism—A style of art where a definite mood or feeling is depicted.

243

Fantasy Art—Artwork that is meant to look unreal, strange, or dreamlike.

foreground—The part in an artwork that seems near or close.

form—A three-dimensional design.

free form—A free-flowing, imaginative shape.

geometric shapes—Shapes that have smooth edges.

horizontal—A line that goes from side to side.

illusion—A misleading image.

imagination—Creative ability.

intermediate colors—Colors that are made by mixing a primary color and a secondary color. Red orange, red violet, blue green, blue violet, yellow orange, and yellow green are intermediate colors.

landscape—Artwork that depicts an outdoor scene.

line—A mark made by a moving point.

mixed media—Artwork made up of different materials or techniques.

mobile—A sculpture with parts that move by air currents.

model—A person who poses for an artist.

montage—A composite picture made by combining several separate pictures.

mosaic—Artwork in which a larger scene is composed of small pieces of color.

movement—The rhythmic qualities of a design.

mural—A large artwork created or displayed on a wall.

negative space—Empty space in a design.

neutral colors—Brown, black, white, and gray.

nonobjective—A style of art where the main ideas or feelings come from the design created with colors, lines, and shapes. It does not depict objects or scenes.

opaque—Not transparent.

original—Artwork that looks very different from other artwork.

overlap—One part that covers some of another part.

pattern—Lines, colors, or shapes repeated over and over in a planned way. A model or guide for making something.

perspective—The extent to which the shapes of objects and distances between them look familiar or correct.

Pop Art—A style of art that uses everyday objects as the subject.

portrait—Artwork that shows the face of a person.

positive space—The actual shapes or figures in a design.

pose—A specific position of the body.

primary colors—Colors from which other colors can be made. Red, blue, and yellow are primary colors.

print—To press and lift something with ink or paint on it.

profile—The side view of something.

proportion—The size, location, or amount of something as compared to something else.

radial—Lines or shapes that come out from a center point.

Realism—A style of artwork that shows objects or scenes as they look in everyday life.

relief—Something that stands out from a flat background.

repetition—The repeated use of the same design elements.

Renaissance—A time in European history (1400–1600) after the Middle Ages. Artists during this time discovered many new ways to create things.

rhythm—A repetition of design elements to create a visual balance.

Romantic—A style of artwork in which the main ideas are to show adventures, imaginary events, faraway places, or strong feelings.

secondary colors—Colors that can be mixed from two primary colors. Orange, green, and purple are secondary colors.

shade—The darkness of colors. A color mixed with black.

shape—The outline edge or flat surface of a form.

space—An empty place or area.

stencil—A flat material with a cutout design.

still life—An artwork that consists of nonliving objects.

style—An artist's personal way of creating art.

symmetry—Parts arranged the same way on both sides.

technique—A special way to create artwork.

texture—The way something feels or the way it looks like it feels.

three-dimensional—Artwork that can be measured three ways: height, width, and depth.

tint—A light color. A color mixed with white.

transparent—Transmitting light.

two-dimensional—Artwork that is flat and can be measured in two ways: height and width.

unity—The quality of having all parts look like they belong.

value—The lightness or darkness of a color.

variety—Having differences.

vertical—A line that runs up and down.

warm colors—Colors that remind people of warm things. Red, yellow, and orange are warm colors.

References

Aikman, L. M. (1991, November). Looking/learning: Edward Hopper: Images of solitude. *School Arts*, 27–30.

Art for Bangor elementary schools. (1976). Bangor, ME: Bangor School Department.

Bernstein, M. (1992, November). Meet the masters. Henri Matisse made collages with colored paper. *Spark*, 8–9.

Bernstein, M. (1992, July). Meet the masters. Georgia O'Keeffe painted flowers close up. *Spark*, 8–9.

Bohm-Duchen, M., & Cook, J. (1988). *Understanding modern art.* Tulsa: EDC.

Canady, J. (1959). *Mainstreams of modern art.* New York: Simon & Schuster.

Chapman, L. (1985). *Discover art.* Worcester, MA: Davis.

Crayola creativity program. (1987). Easton, PA: Binney & Smith.

Derby, M. C. (1993, April). 1st-grade Matisses. *Arts & Activities*, 18–19.

Dictionary of artists and sculptors. (1970). New York: Pyramid Books.

Doorneck, R. (1992, September). Looking/learning: Winslow Homer: Watercolor and wilderness. *School Arts*, 33–36.

Doorneck, R. (1994, March). Looking/learning: M.C. Escher beyond the craft. *School Arts*, 25–28.

Hellwege, P. (1993, December). Looking/learning: Vincent van Gogh visiting near Arles. *School Arts*, 31–34.

Herzog, M. (1991, September). Looking/learning: Intimacy in pastel: Mary Cassatt. *School Arts*, 31–34.

Jared, A. (1997, March). Looking/learning: Georgia O'Keeffe connected to nature. *School Arts*, 25–28.

Johnson, M. M. Clip art: American Gothic. *Arts & Activities.*

Johnson, M. M. Clip art: Dancer with Red Stockings. *Arts & Activities.*

Kinghorn, H., Badman J., & Lewis-Spicer, L. (1991). *Let's meet famous artists.* Minneapolis, MN: T. S. Denison.

Krull, K. (1995). *Lives of the artists.* New York: Harcourt Brace.

Losos, C. M. (1993, December). Looking/learning: Henri Rousseau carnival evening. *School Arts*, 21–24.

Michael, J. A. (1980, February). Studio art experience: the heart of education. *Art Education*, 15–19.

Miller, R. (1993, August). Meet the masters: Paul Gauguin painted objects in unusual colors. *Spark*, 8–9.

Nerreau, J. C. (1992, May/June). Meet the masters: Amedeo Modigliani was a painter. *Spark*, 8–9.

Nerreau, J. C. (1992, February). Meet the masters: Artist Romare Bearden made collages. *Spark*, 8–9.

Nerreau, J. C. (1993, January/February). Meet the masters: Jackson Pollack made "action" paintings. *Spark*, 8–9.

Nerreau, J. C. (1993, April). Meet the masters: Jasper Johns turned numbers into art. *Spark*, 8–9.

Nerreau, J. C. (1992, September/October). Meet the masters: Marc Chagall painted stories. *Spark*, 10–11.

Niceley, H. T. (1990, November). Looking/learning: Christina's World: Andrew Wyeth. *School Arts*, 27–30.

Niceley, H. T. (1992, March). Paul Klee's Twittering Machine. *School Arts*, 31.

Raboff, E. (1988). *Paul Gauguin: Art for children*. New York: Harper & Row.

Rodriguez, S. (1988). *Art smart*. Englewood Cliffs, NJ: Prentice Hall.

Slemmer, P. (1992, October). Autumn leaves an experiment in cubism. *Arts & Activities*, 62–63.

Stricker, S. (1982). *The anti-coloring book of masterpieces*. New York: Henry Holt.

The art book. (1994). London: Phaidon Press.

The Shorewood art reference guide. (1996). New York: Shorewood Reproductions.

Tomlinson, G., & Bassett, B. (1996, October). Looking/learning: Three musicians. *School Arts*.

Toon, P. (1993, March). Meet the masters: Edgar Degas drew and painted people in motion. *Spark*, 8–9.

Toon, P. (1993, July). Meet the masters: Winslow Homer painted watercolor seascapes. *Spark*, 8–9.

Venzia, M. (1988). *Getting to know the world's greatest artists: Da Vinci*. Chicago: Children's Press.

Venzia, M. (1988). *Getting to know the world's greatest artists: Mary Cassatt*. Chicago: Children's Press.

Venzia, M. (1988). *Getting to know the world's greatest artists: Monet*. Chicago: Children's Press.

Venzia, M. (1988). *Getting to know the world's greatest artists: Picasso*. Chicago: Children's Press.

Venzia, M. (1988). *Getting to know the world's greatest artists: Rembrandt*. Chicago: Children's Press.

Venzia, M. (1988). Getting to know the world's greatest artists: van Gogh. Chicago: Children's Press.

What's going on here? Be a critic, think like a detective. (1994, October). *School Arts*.

Wolf, A. D. (1984). *Mommy, it's a Renoir*. Altoona, PA: Parent Child Press.

Index